From Home School to College
The African American Experience

From Home School to College
The African American Experience

Taj'ullah X. Sky Lark, PhD

Wise Womyn Write
2015

Published by

WISE WOMYN WRITE
P.O. Box 14
Kent's Store, Virginia 23084

Copyright © 2014 by Taj'ullah X. Sky Lark, PhD

All rights reserved. No part of this book may be reproduced in any form or by any means, electronic or mechanical, including information storage and retrieval systems without written permission from the publisher.

Photo Credits: Skylar P. Lark
Book Design by: Taj'ullah X. Sky Lark, PhD

Library of Congress Control Number: 2015921025

ISBN-13: 978-0692575772
ISBN-10: 0692575774

CONTENTS

Preface vii

Chapters

I. Brief Historical Overview of the Black Educational Journey in America... p. 1

II. Brief Background on Homeschooling... p. 5

III. Failing Public School System and the Notion of Homeschooling... p. 9

IV. Socialization in Education... p.13

V. African American Homeschooling... p.17

VI. College Student Transition... p. 21

VII. Homeschoolers Transition to College... p.27

VIII. Gap in the Knowledge Base on African American Homeschoolers Transition to PWIs... p.31

IX. Purpose of the Research Study... p.35

X. Research Design... p.39

XI. Analysis of the Findings... p.47

XII. Conclusion... p.83

Table 1 Participants... p.93

References p. 95

Dedication

I dedicate this book to my Husband Skylar and five Daughters Zenzile, Laxmi, Selu, Somalia, and Xuxa. You are all a blessing. To my dear Father Frederick, Grandmother Edna, and Sister Karen, may you rest in peace. I love you all.

Preface

There is an expectation that 50% of today's homeschoolers will apply to four-year colleges and universities across the nation, with an undetermined number of African American homeschooled applicants (Bielick, 2008; Egelko & Tucker, 2008; Maxwell & Maxwell, 2008; Ray, 2008, 2011). Current research has shown that the transition experiences of homeschooled students, in general, is typical of non-homeschooled students transitioning into college, and they adjust well within the college social life (Bolle, Wessel, & Mulvihill, 2007; Kraznow, 2005; Ray, 2009; White et al., 2007).

Empirical research shows that homeschooled students have few transition issues and are equally, if not more, academically prepared for college than non-homeschooled students are (Ray, 2005, 2009; Van Pelt, 2003). Duggan (2010), Goodman (2008), and Lisle (2006) found that the homeschool educational background contributed, in part, to the success of these students in college. However, the current published research is limited, with the focus on the experiences of White homeschoolers and the bulk of research resting in the doctoral dissertations. There is paucity in research on the experiences of African American homeschooled students who transition into college.

A plethora of research on the transition of non-homeschooled first-year African American college students identified challenges with social and academic preparedness (Barnett, 2004; Brown, Morning, & Watkins, 2005; Engstrom, & Tinto, 2008; Hausmann, Ye,

Schofield, & Woods, 2009; Sledge, 2012). Assumptions should not be made that similar challenges are, or are not, present for African American college students who were homeschooled, making an investigation into this emerging population entering colleges and universities an important contribution to the knowledge base.

Past and current research have documented the continued challenges that African American students experience transitioning into predominately White colleges and universities, African American males in particular (Antonio et al., Chang, Milem, 2005; Cruce, 2006; Harper, 2006; Flowers, 2007; Harvey & Harvey, 2005; Harvey, 2008; Levin et al., 2007; Moore & Owens, 2008; Palmer, 2008; Strayhorn, 2008). Some of these challenges are lack of resources, lack of support, discrimination, stereotyping, no voice, Eurocentric-centered curriculum, and inhospitable learning environments.

While the majority of documented homeschoolers in the United States are predominantly White, the African American homeschoolers are documented as one of the fastest growing homeschool populations over the last 5 years (Ray, 2011). With the increase in the numbers of homeschooled African Americans, and undetermined numbers applying to and attending colleges and universities, engaging in research that explores the preparedness of this newly emerging population may be useful in addressing any potential challenges these students encounter at PWIs. Additionally, institutes of higher education would have the unique opportunity to learn from the collected data about what variables come into play that may be attributed to the success of the African American homeschooler population, which may in turn inspire and/or require curriculum, institutional, or policy changes in the future.

Research exploring the transition experiences of formerly homeschooled African American students provides insight that will enable higher education administrators, student affairs practitioners, faculty, and homeschooling parents, to address the challenges that this emerging student population may encounter. Research exploring the transition experiences of formerly homeschooled African American students also sheds light on what pedagogy, compulsory curriculum, socialization strategies, and support are being implemented to accredit the successful transition of African American homeschooled students into Predominantly White Institutions.

There is a gap in the research aimed at exploring the college transition experiences of homeschooled African Americans into PWIs. The last 25 years of research on the college academic achievements of formally homeschooled students conducted locally, statewide, and nationally, have consistently shown that the measure of academic aptitude of these students is equal to, if not higher than, those of non-homeschooled students (Ray, 2009). Researchers Belfield, 2005; Bolle et al., 2007; Chatmon, 2006; Clemente, 2006; Kranzow, 2005; Qaqish, 2007; White et al., 2007 proclaim that formerly homeschooled college students are successful meeting the rigors of a college-level curriculum and the transition at institutions of higher education with very few uncommon challenges. However, past research has been rudimentary, demographically limited, and anecdotal with research subjects being predominantly White homeschoolers (Nemer, 2000). Review of past research on the transition experiences of homeschoolers into college has failed to chronicle specifically how African Americans transition into college. Past research has been limited and anecdotal with research subjects predominantly comprised of White homeschoolers. According to Banks (2004), the current public educational system in America is based on the European experience, belief systems, theory, values, and history. Because Eurocentric focused curriculum marginalizes the history and experiences of other ethnic groups, it hinders positive transformative learning and creates barriers that have detrimental effects on how minority groups strive in education.

Research on the transition experiences of African American college students attending PWIs of higher learning has documented significant challenges these students face and identified this student population as at risk for departure (Brown, Morning, & Watkins, 2005; Cruce, 2006; Sledge, 2012; Ye, Schofield, & Woods, 2009). Considering the established research on the transition experiences of African Americans attending PWIs, expanding the scope to include the transition experiences of homeschooled African American college students into PWIs begins to fill the gap within the knowledge base.

There is a gap in the research aimed at exploring the college transition experiences of homeschooled African Americans into Predominantly White Institutions (PWIs). The past research has been rudimentary, demographically limited, and anecdotal with predominantly White homeschoolers as research subjects. In 2013, Dr. Taj'ullah Sky Lark conducted a first of its kind qualitative study that explored the transition experiences of eight homeschooled African American students into PWIs guided by Tinto's student transition theory. The qualitative study found the transition experience of homeschooled African Americans into college and university learning environments of PWIs consisted of typical transitional experiences common to most college students learning the culture of a new environment. This study also found that while homeschooled African Americans faced similar transition challenges as identified by established empirical research on the experience of African American college students attending PWIs, these challenges were not barriers to their academic success or retention.

Chapter I

Brief Historical Overview of the Black Educational Journey in America

In order to conceptualize the importance and necessity of this research study in the field of higher education, one must consider historical aspects that have and continue to play a significant role in the educational journey of African Americans into higher education, concomitant with homeschooling and the rise in African American homeschoolers and their transition into PWIs.

Prior to the Civil War, most African Americans were not educated, since for the most part, it was illegal and African Americans seeking education took a high risk if caught trying to read or write (Tozer, Senese, & Violas, 2006). Blacks nonetheless recognized the value of an education and endured life threatening efforts to educate their own children in secret schools, churches, and in rare moments offered by a sympathetic slave master or a member of his staff (Brown & Yates, 2005; Fleming, 1981). Moreover, the dominant culture saw no importance in schooling African Americans, and less importance in schooling women, especially African American women (Tozer et al., 2006). Although views would slowly shift towards schooling White women, these views were not entertained about the schooling or education of African Americans for some time (Tozer et al., 2006).

Slave Codes enacted in the 1600s and Black Code Laws enacted initially around 1865 in the United States played a role in the disenfranchisement of Blacks and equal access to education (Franklin & Moss, 2000). These codes varied from state to state, but united in the common purpose of denying the civil rights of Blacks (Brown & Yates, 2005; Wallenstein, 2004, 2010). Jim Crow laws facilitated the disenfranchisement of Blacks in every aspect of life (Fleming, 1981; Woodward, 1987).

Plessy v. Ferguson (1896) would affirm and establish the framework of segregation which provided the "the constitutional, as well as legal, bedrock for the entire system of racial segregation in the South" (Samuels, 2004, p. 3). With the passage of the Morrill Act of 1890, many public colleges for Negroes were established; however, there were no specific laws in place that directly barred Blacks from traditionally White universities (*Morrill Act* 1890, Ch. 841, 26 Stat. 417; 7 U.S.C. Sec. 323). No references were made in the provisions of higher education that pertained to race, even though most states had erected state-funded universities by the end of Reconstruction (Peer, 1982).

The Supreme Court handed down a decision in Sipuel v. Oklahoma State Board of Regents, 1948 [*Sipuel v. Board of Regents*, 332 U.S. 631 (1948)], that severely narrowed the state's ability to maintain segregated law schools. By June 1950, the Court had ruled against segregation in a follow-up case from Texas, *Sweatt v. Painter*, 339 U.S. 629 (1950), and at the University of Oklahoma *McLaurin v. Oklahoma State Regents*, 339 U.S. 637 (1950). These court cases ruled that the segregation of the plaintiffs by state-funded institutions of higher education racially stigmatized and deprived them of an equal educational experience.

The landmark Supreme Court case *Brown v. Board of Education Topeka* 347 U.S. 483 (1954) unanimously affirmed that separate educational facilities are unconstitutional and inherently unequal. This decision would begin the desegregation of schools and the right to equal opportunity to an education. During integration, the social implications of the *Brown v. Board* decision would pave the way for a new phase of the Civil Rights Movement and "equal access" for children in compulsory studies in desegregated learning environments. However, African American students would experience a tumultuous educational journey consisting of extreme resistance from the dominant culture, from racial discrimination and riots to physical violence, in defense of their rights for equal access and equal opportunity for educational success (Cottrol, Diamond, & Ware, 2003; Cushman, 2004; Kluger, 1977; Martin, 1998; Patterson, 2001; Wallenstein, 2008). To date, African American students still contend with teacher attitudes, barriers to equitable access to quality education, underprepared teachers, insensitive curricula, and an unyielding steady decline in educational achievement within K-12 public school systems (Gordon, 2006; Kunjufu, 2005a; Tyson, 2003) and predominately White colleges and universities (Antonio, Chang, & Milem, 2005; Flowers, 2007; Harvey, 2008; Harvey & Harvey, 2005; Levin, Belfield, Muennig, & Rouse, 2007; Moore & Owens, 2008; Sky Lark, 2012; Swail, 2003).

    The challenges unique to the transition of African American college students at PWIs have been established in higher education, providing insight to student affairs professionals, counselors, and faculty on the student population (Flowers, 2007; Harvey & Harvey, 2005; Harvey, 2008; Levin et al., 2007; Moore & Owens, 2008; Massey, Charles, Lundy, & Fischer, 2003). With the established knowledge on transition challenges of African American college students at PWIs, the void in research on African American homeschoolers justifies an inquiry into the dynamics of how this emerging student population transitions into college and university environments.

CHAPTER II

Brief Background on Homeschooling

The notion of "homeschooling" is not a new phenomenon in American history. In fact, prior to compulsory education, homeschooling was the primary form of education in America during the 1700s and into the early 1900s for the greater populace, with formal schooling only for the children of the elite (DiStefano, Kjell, & Silverman, 2004). Over the centuries, dismay with the educational system, concerns of lost values and morality, poor learning environments with under-skilled teachers, coupled with political agendas underpinning education reform caused many to turn to educating their children in hopes of providing a better opportunity for academic success (Bielick, 2008; Bolle et al., 2007; Fields-Smith & Williams 2009; Ray, 2004b, 2001, 2005, 2009).

The homeschooled population today constitutes more than 2.5 to 3 million students in the United States and is a segment of society that has not only grown in numbers but in sophistication (Ray, 2011). Home education is arguably the fastest growing form of education in the United States compared to public and private institutional schooling. Results of Ray's (2003, 2004b, 2005, 2009, 2011) research on reasons for homeschooling included: 1) individualized curriculum; 2) non-traditional pedagogical approaches; 3) guided social interactions; 4) teaching set values; 5) promiscuity in public school systems; and, 6) public schools becoming physically and mentally unhealthy. The participants of these small research studies were predominantly White, limited in scope, and isolated. Table 1 reports the results of a parent survey conducted by the U.S. Department of Education National Center for Education Statistics (2007) which indicated the various reasons why parents have chosen to home educate their children verse have them enrolled in public or private schools.

While there has been a decline in opposition to homeschooling, it is not free of its critics who argue that parents are neither equipped to teach their children the standard K-12 curriculum adequately nor able to prepare them to become critical thinkers with the necessary skills to be productive members of a pluralistic society (Hudak, 2003). Lubienski (2000), a critic of homeschooling, contended that homeschooling is not democratic education. Lubienski regarded homeschools as a weak link in maintaining a democratic society with shared morals. Other criticism included the lack of monetary financial support to local schools systems, lack of curriculum oversight or comparable coursework (Rothermel, 2003). However, much of the argument against homeschooling focused on stereotypes rooted in scholars' personal biases rather than on empirical research (Rothermel, 2003). Pfleger (2003) contended that the statistical research conducted on homeschooling was flawed and limited in scope. Nemer (2002) argued that the samplings of some of the research was too small, selective, and based on predominantly White participants.

CHAPTER III

Failing Public School System and the Notion of Homeschooling

According to the U.S. Department of Education, each day nearly 7,000 high school students become dropouts, adding up to 1.3 million students annually. In October 2007, approximately 3.3 million 16- through 24-year olds did not earn a high school diploma or alternative credentials (Cataldi, Laird, & Ramani, 2009).

The government's educational agenda has gone from Civil Rights efforts that focused on the desegregation of schools and equal education to standards and testing, none of which closed the achievement gap or desegregated schools (Spring, 2010). Many 21st century students from families with economic challenges dealing with additional discriminations and societal barriers may have the propensity to achieve equal access to high quality education for the marginalized. However, it is still evident in the nation along with a digital divide between the poor and the privileged that the achievement gap between Whites and Blacks is increasing (Howey & Zimpher, 2007). The public school system has returned to being stratified due to the socioeconomics of capitalism, with public school systems playing a direct role in maintaining and recreating barriers that establish economic and class division with hints of social reproduction for minorities in general, and males in particular (Spring, 2010).

Failing Public School System and the Notion of Homeschooling

Some scholars believe the root cause of failed school systems and programs in education are due in part to the trend of merely adopting a standard style to lead all types of schools (Birnbaum, 2004). Not only do teaching styles have to be revisited, but leadership styles as well, in order to be progressive and applicable to the needs of the students, faculty and administration, institution, and all its stakeholders (Birnbaum, 2004). Hunt (2007) suggested that successful fundamental reforms should be institutionalized instead of eliminated with each new administration. Hunt (2007) further stated that the stakeholders must have more involvement and have access to information from political leaders to stay aware of current studies, trends, strategies, and setbacks so citizens can contribute comprehensive feedback for consideration. Some stakeholders have taken the fate of their children's education into their own hands through electing the option to homeschool.

Darling-Hammond (2007), Collom (2005), and Ray (2011) proclaimed that many students were being taught by under prepared young teachers who lacked experience and 21st century teaching skills, by career changers who lacked pedagogy, and older educators who were stuck in "tradition" and authoritative, behaviorist teaching styles. Wise (2007) noted that innovative educators found themselves limited and restricted, teaching in outmoded school systems that used cookie-cutter, factory model teaching and learning standards.

Surveys conducted by Ray (2003, 2004a, 2004b, 2005) with homeschooling parents, stated reasons for a rise in homeschooling as religion, failed school systems, bullying, poor curriculum, overcrowding, socialization, frustrations with government involvement in education, never ending education reforms, failure of No Child Left Behind, standardized testing, and teacher/student ratios. Brint (2006) stated that the issue of socialization is a reason many have chosen to homeschool. According to Brint, socialization is the process of becoming competent in ways of behaving within the dominant culture's social norms and standards through enculturation that are passed down from one generation to the next. Brint further asserted that socialization in education trains students in norms expected of them within a controlled learning environment they will internalize and transfer outside of the classroom into their communities, employment, and the society at large (2006).

This conditioning begins early and is most profound in K-12 education, and documented as an issue for homeschooling parents according to qualitative and quantitative research studies conducted by Princiotta, Bielick, & Chapman (2004) and Ray (2011). Other reasons have been documented for choosing to homeschool as well. Approximately 30% chose to homeschool due to their child having special needs; 72% for religious beliefs; and more than 85% because of peer pressure, school safety, drugs, and alcohol (Princiotta et al., 2004).

CHAPTER IV

Socialization in Education

The socialization of children has been one of the most pertinent concerns of homeschooling parents and opponents of homeschooling. While opponents like Apple (2006) believed that religious based homeschooling limits the cultural and intellectual diversity of learning, and that public schools provided the best environment for learning about the world, Reich's (2002) concerns were whether homeschooling's customized learning would subsequently diminish the pluralistic democracy of American society.

Bowditch (2003) questioned the lack of socialization of homeschoolers due to over-protective parents. Homeschooling parents, however, appeared to be more concerned with the socialization of their children through a prescribed values system not in keeping with their own (Ray, 2000b, 2005, 2009). Parents did not want their children subjected to tracking and social reproduction that will disenfranchise, and/or limit their child's full potential and opportunity for academic success (Bielick, 2008; Bolle et al., 2007; Fields-Smith & Williams 2009). Areas of concern were:

Behavior Conformity: Long-term training by an authoritative entity to control freethinking and the suppression of actions deemed unacceptable by the dominant culture. The process of controlling the masses through behavioral conformity involves the body, its language, its mechanical actions, the tools used, and how it is adorned (Brint, 2006). Examples of behavioral conformity in compulsory education include assigned seating, asking permission to go to the restroom, asking permission to sharpen pencils, lining up, walking down hallways in a single file, handing assignments in on time, dressing according to school code, and attendance. Compliance to these disciplines reap rewards for good behavior, teacher's pet, while non-compliance results in behavioral modification, or some level of punishment where privileges are taken away (Brint, 2006).

Moral Conformity: Training that consists of character building that understands, internalizes, and produces actions that are in line with the belief system, ethics, virtues, and values of the dominant culture. Some qualities that moral conformity training attempts to develop include cooperation, self-respect, respect for others, truthfulness, humility, development of conscience and awareness of consequence, civic duty, and sharing (Brint, 2006). Some examples of moral conformity in education are following school rules, obeying the teacher, respecting authority, classroom walls decorated with historic or religious figures that represent courage, national heroes, compassion, and/or honesty (Brint, 2006).

It is possible to teach moral conformity without reference to any specific religion according to Shearer, author of the 1907 *New York Times* article entitled, "Character Building in the School." He stated children could learn not to break the rules without reference made to any denomination so as not to give sectarian instruction in public schools (Shearer, 1907).

Cultural Conformity: Training in the traditional values, views, and styles of the dominant culture. Some of the core values that make up cultural conformity are personal achievement, hard work, civic responsibility, efficiency and practicality, progress, patriotism, religious value, competition, science rationality, racial and group superiority. These core values not only reflect the cultural logic of the dominant culture, but also the logic of a particular time and place (Brint, 2006). These social norms are internalized via sanctions to eventually become a part of an individual's personality. Some examples of cultural conformity are saluting the flag, being addressed as girls and boys, getting good grades, volunteering, the exposure to the dominant cultures' holidays, and the following of acceptable trends (Brint, 2006).

The purpose of integrating social skills into curriculum serves many agendas thought to be in the best interest of the country. Some examples are the transmission of culture, social control, social placement in the form of "tracking," as a cultural conservative force, and "cooling out" (handling of "failures" in the student body). Durkheim (1923-1961) stated that the development of habits and conduct are the most important task of schooling, most importantly the aptitude of self-control. Brint (2006) stated that schools specialize in the creation and preparation of people for adult life who can adapt to environments that are impersonal. While the mission of most schools is to produce law abiding, well-rounded productive adults, respect has become the ethical focus in contemporary schooling (Brint, Contreras, & Matthews, 2001).

The research of Brint et al. (2001) and Brint (2006) found that social skills were embedded into curriculum in a variety of creative ways such as the learning of patriotic songs, sports teams developing competitive skills, cheerleading supportive skills, clubs for getting along with others, segregated gym and health classes by gender, mandatory reading lists to instill the consequences of right and wrong, answering questions correctly, role playing to develop listening skills, and being responsible for classroom tasks (Brint, 2006).

Many homeschooling parents believed that they could avoid this type of socialization by educating their own children (Bielick, 2008; Bolle et al., 2007; Fields-Smith & Williams 2009; Ray, 2000b, 2001, 2005; Ray, 2009). However, what happens when African American homeschooled students within campus environments at PWIs struggle with diversity issues and high dropout rates within their first year of attendance? Research on the transition of African American homeschooled students into college is necessary to begin to explore these avenues.

CHAPTER V

African American Homeschooling

According to Fulbright (2005), the homeschooling population of African Americans has risen since 1999. Ray (2011) supported Fulbright's findings that African Americans were one of the fastest growing minority homeschooled populations in the United States just within the last 5 years. Apple (2006) affirmed that African Americans are one of the fastest growing homeschool populations in comparison to Latino and other minority groups in the America, but questioned the reasoning behind Blacks choosing to homeschool, and even more so, the capabilities from intellectual to financial in order to homeschool successfully. Apple suggested that traditionally oppressed people are incapable of educating their children properly in order to be successful in society (2006).

A single research study conducted by Fields-Smith and Williams (2009), published in the *Urban Review* is currently the only research study available on African American homeschoolers. The Fields-Smith and Williams study focused on African American parents' motivations that attributed to their decision to homeschool their children. Two questions guided the Fields-Smith and Williams (2009) two-year study:

1. What self-reported factors influenced Black parents' decisions to homeschool their children?

2. What challenges do Black families experience in implementing their homeschool practices?

The theoretical framework utilized to analyze African American parents' decision to homeschool their children was based on Bronfenbrenner's (1986) socio-ecological model and Hoover-Dempsey & Sandler's (1997) construction model. A qualitative study with a phenomenological approach, the researchers conducted individual interviews with parents, as well as collected data through surveys and focus groups.

Participants in the study were selected by community nomination and word of mouth from individuals aware of African American homeschooling parents in their neighborhoods in the state of Georgia. Twenty-four parents participated in this research study. Fields-Smith and Williams' (2009) findings provided insight on the African American homeschool movement, which documents important information on what led these parents to decide to homeschool, pedagogy and curriculum utilized, challenges they faced as homeschooling parents, and demographic data.

While the study identified that African American parents shared similar reasons as White homeschooling parents for choosing to homeschool such as failing school system, poor school environment, and religion, African Americans prioritized their motives differently. Their primary concerns were that school environments are destructive to the development of Black children, lacked cultural sensitivity, and deemed racially discriminative with a "one-size- fits-all" pedagogy (Fields-Smith & Williams, 2009).

African American homeschooling parents of sons also voiced their concerns about labeling and the overrepresentation of African American males in special education, which has been identified by scholars in the field of education (Anderson, Howard, & Graham, 2007; Artiles, Harry, Reschly, & Chinn 2002; Artiles, Kozleski, Trent, Osher, & Ortiz, 2010; Blanchett & Shealey, 2005; Decker, Dona, & Christensen, 2007; Hosp & Reschley, 2004; Klingner & Edwards, 2006; Kunjufu, (2005b); O'Conner & Fernandez, 2006; Shealey & Lue, 2006). Public school systems are focused on behavior modification and measuring the learning capabilities of minority students especially using deficit models that target minorities and African American males in particular (Klingner & Edwards, 2006), motivating many African Americans to opt to educate their children (Fields-Smith & Williams, 2009).

Fields-Smith and Williams' (2009) study also revealed that the demographics outside of race spanned single-parent households and low-income households to two-parent households and college-educated parents with mid- to high-income ranges. Most found it important to utilize an Afrocentric curriculum and integrate African and African American history in various disciplines to nurture their child's identity and self-esteem, as well as the histories of other minority cultures (Fields-Smith & Williams, 2009).

The information provided by Fields-Smith and Williams (2009) is a tremendous contribution to the scant knowledge base on the African American homeschool movement, although small in scope, is the beginning of the efforts of scholars attempting to bridge the gap in the area of the African American homeschool movement and provides the opportunity for further research. Based on the data collected, many of the children whose parents participated in Fields-Smith & Williams' (2009) research study were of the age to begin application to college, or already attending, as will many other African American homeschoolers across the nation.

CHAPTER VI
College Student Transition

Transition denotes the adjustment from one educational learning environment to another (Tinto, 1988). First year students at four-year institutions across the nation will experience transitioning. According to Tinto (1988), during this time most students will experience academic adjustments with curriculum, course loads, new peers and instructors, adjustments with making new friends, a new environment, adapting to a new culture, as well as how to maneuver through the institutional bureaucracy and complex administrative structures of college. Students having difficulty with academic or social adjustments, as well as problems with understanding the complex administrative structures of their college or university will struggle with transitioning (Braxton, Hirschy, & McClendon, 2004; Tinto, 2006).

The first year of a student's college education will determine how that student will move forward to degree attainment (Nora, Barlow, & Crisp, 2005). Nora et al., (2005) contended that certain components must be in place for a student to be successful, such as academic preparedness, support, and acclamation to the college culture. Researchers theorize that students lacking academic and financial support and/or having difficulty making social adjustments will fail to transition into their new environment (Tinto, 1993). Research has shown that African Americas have historically struggled with transitioning into institutions of higher education in America (Terenzini et al., 1994). This research explored how homeschooled African American students transition into Predominantly White Institutions.

Transition Challenges of African Americans in Higher Education

Allen, Bonous-Hammarth, and Teranishi, (2006) indicated that the problem of diversity in the 21st century is rapidly expanding alongside a stubbornly persistent status quo and power inequalities by race, ethnicity, gender, sexual orientation, class, language, citizenship, and region. Allen et al. (2006) asserted that African American students face numerous learning challenges in a society where power inequalities such as class, race, ethnicity, gender, and sexual orientation continue to thrive and directly affect transition into higher education. Antonio et al. (2005) believed that there were serious repercussions of a mono-cultural faculty serving a multicultural student body with a singular curricular perspective. According to Steele (1997, 2010), African American students still contend with stereotyping which threatens intellectual identity and performance.

There is a consensus among researchers (Ancis, Sedlacek, & Mohr, 2000; Antonio et al., 2005; Flowers, 2007; Grant-Vallone, et al, 2003-2004; Harvey & Harvey, 2005; Harvey, 2008; Gordon, 2006; Karemera, Reuben, & Sillah, 2003; Kunjufu, 2005a; Levin et al.,

2007; Moore & Owens, 2008; Sky Lark, 2012; Steele, 1997; Swail, 2003; Tyson, 2003) that African American students continue to face challenges at PWIs. Some of these challenges are teacher attitudes, barriers to equitable access to quality education, under-prepared teachers, insensitive curricula, and an unyielding steady decline in educational achievement within K-12 public and private school systems and PWIs.

Studies on the transition, retention, and matriculation of African American students documented the interview and survey responses from participating students on their experience and stressors at PWIs. The results of this research documented the experiences and stressors as isolation, professor bias, biased grading practices, and financial difficulty. Study participants also stated experiencing racism from White administrators, faculty, as well as other students. Also of note was concern with the lack of African American professors; accusation by peers of "acting White;" discriminatory institutional policies; and insensitivity of White advisors and counselors (Adams, 2005; Anglin & Wade, 2007; Antonio et al., 2005; Chang & Demyan, 2007, 2005; Flowers, 2007; Greer & Chwalisz, 2007; Harvey & Harvey, 2005; Harvey, 2008; Levin et al., 2007; Moore & Owens, 2008; Parker, M. & Flowers, L.A. 2003; Reid & Radhakrishnan, 2003; Negga, Applewhite, Livingston, 2007; Smith & Hopkins, 2004).

June, Cluny, and Gear (1990) conducted a quantitative study on African Americans attending PWIs, which resulted in finding that there were major issues with African American students transitioning into the already established culture of PWI college environments and the psycho-emotional effects of social isolation. Cuyjet (2006a) found African American males maintained one of the highest rates in failed academic success, transition, and retention issues. Other scholars in the field supported Cuyjet's findings regarding the challenges of African American males in PWIs as having the tendency to require more than 4 years to matriculate, not academically prepared for college level course work, and lacking good study skills. The findings also documented that African American males tended not to engage in college activities that were required educationally and deemed necessary to acquire a certain level of social capital for simplifying transitioning and collegiate navigation (Bonner, II, & Bailey 2006; Cruce, Wolniak, Seifert, & Pascarella, 2006; Harper, 2006; Kuh & Hu, 2005; Nelson Laird et al., 2007; Palmer & Hilton, 2008; Strayhorn, 2008).

Two hundred and fifty African American undergraduate students participated in a longitudinal quantitative study conducted by Nasim, Roberts, Hamell, & Young (2005) to investigate ways race affected how African Americans achieved in PWIs. Nasim et al. (2005) administered the Multidimensional Inventory of Black Identity designed by Sellers, Rowley, Tabbye, Shelton, & Smith, (1997) to study participants. The results indicated that racial identity for African Americans significantly impacted their academic performance in PWIs. A qualitative research study conducted by Fries-Britt and Turner (2001) investigating the challenges of African American students attending a PWI with 15 African American participants, eight women and six males, established three themes: racial stereotypes; race-based insults on physical characteristics; and challenges to intellectual competence.

Qualitative research conducted by Kirkland (1998) to identify the stress experienced by African American undergraduate nursing students attending a PWI concluded these students had experienced lack of African American role models or support from White faculty. Solorzano (2000) conducted a qualitative study on the racial dynamics on PWI campuses as experienced by African American students. Participants expressed being stereotyped negatively regarding their academic propensity by White students and faculty; racial tensions in and outside the classroom; and feelings of segregation, all of which significantly affected their self-esteem and academic performance. The result of this study aligned with the results of studies conducted by Steele (1995, 1997, and 2010) on "stereotype threat" and African American students internalizing beliefs of inferiority to Whites in the area of intellect. Students from non-dominant groups at PWIs were struggling to strive in a learning environment that continued to utilize mainstream hidden curriculum, further alienating them from their own cultural contributions and experiences within the dominant culture. Their contributions to the class were not as valued as were White students; many times teachers graded their work critically and unfairly with feedback that was negative, discouraging, destructive, and even demeaning (Gay, 2000).

    Research conducted on environmental perceptions of PWIs by Phillips (2005) comparing the perceptions of White and African American students at a predominantly White campus revealed that White students were unaware of the challenges faced by African American students. This study also found that African Americans students felt marginalized, causing them to experience academic difficulty and socialization issues. According to Phillips (2005), these feelings of marginalization seriously affected the retention rates of African Americans. Past and current research documented the continued challenges that African American students experience transitioning into colleges and universities in general and African American males in particular (Cruce, Wolniak, Seifert, & Pascarella, 2006; Flowers, 2007; Harvey, 2008; Palmer & Hilton, 2008; Moore & Owens, 2008; Strayhorn, 2008). Past and current research identified some of these challenges of African American college students at PWIs as lack of resources, lack of support, discrimination, stereotyping, no voice, Eurocentric centered curriculum, and chilly environment.

CHAPTER VII
Homeschoolers Transition to College

The National Home Education Research Institute estimates that between 1.7 million and 2.4 million children were educated at home between the years 2005-2010. Based on this current information, there were approximately 2.5 to 3 million K-12 homeschooled students living in the U.S. in 2012 with 50% attending college (Ray 2003, 2004a, 2004b). It is possible that this rise in homeschooled children has increased the applications to colleges and universities across the nation, many of whom may increasingly be African American. Table 2 shows the rise in documented African American homeschoolers comparative to White homeschoolers in the United States according to the National Center for Education Statistics (2003) and the Parent and Family Involvement in Education Survey of the National Household Education Surveys Program (1999, 2003, 2007, and 2011).

Research on homeschoolers conducted by Jones and Gloeckner (2004) discovered that college and university admissions officers across the United States continued to grapple with how to address a growing population of newly graduated homeschooled students each year. They also affirmed that negative perceptions on behalf of college administrators, teachers, counselors, and even some college students as the biggest transition obstacles homeschoolers face. Jones and Gloeckner (2004) stated the challenges this sub-population experienced and presented to the institution aside from admission policies and technology occurred in student development socialization, academic freedoms, and teaching styles/theories.

According to Ray (2009), universities have rigorous entrance requirements with much of the weight placed on standardized tests, personal essays, letters of recommendation, and high school transcripts. Thus, admissions requirements are no longer the biggest barrier for homeschoolers. Many homeschoolers who have come of age over the recent years are applying directly to four-year institutions (Bolle et al., 2007; Kranzow, 2005; White et al., 2007). Data collected by Ray (2009) in a cross-sectional descriptive study of 11,739 homeschoolers across the United States indicated that homeschoolers were achieving higher than were non-homeschooled students regardless of chosen curriculum, teaching style or family dynamics in regards to college preparedness.

A quantitative study of 25 previously homeschooled college students conducted by Lattibeaudiere (2000) utilizing the Student Adaptation to College Questionnaire (SACQ) developed by Baker & Siryk (1989). SACQ is an instrument that assesses the academic, emotional, and social adjustments of freshmen students at colleges and universities that placed homeschoolers in the 84th percentile for emotional adjustment and the 76th percentile in social adjustment compared to the national standard. Further research by Bolle et al.

(2007) reported that homeschooled students, during their first year of college, would experience transitional issues such as loneliness, meeting others with different values, and dealing with greater independence. Research by Bolle, et al. (2007) was limited to predominantly White homeschoolers. These researchers also sought to determine if experiences of such students corresponded to Tinto's (1982, 1993) theory of student departure. The qualitative study found little distinction between the transitional experiences of home schooled and traditionally educated students.

Research utilizing the Rosenberg Self Esteem Scale (1965) by Holder (2001) also reported that homeschoolers adjust to college environments no differently than do non-homeschoolers. Other research instruments utilized by scholars such as the 1991 College Adjustment Scale (CAS) to measure the socialization and adjustment of homeschoolers in college settings presented similar results (Brower et al., 2007).

Bolle et al.'s (2007) qualitative study of six previously homeschooled college students attending a Midwestern college in the U.S. focused on the transition of the study participants' first year showed that homeschoolers experienced similar common transition experiences as non-homeschooled college students such as loneliness, independence, and making new friends. The research on homeschoolers and their transition into college has been limited; participants were predominantly White with qualitative and quantitative studies small in sample size (Bolle et al., 2007; White et al. 2007).

CHAPTER VIII
Gap in the Knowledge Base on African American Homeschoolers Transition to PWIs

There is a gap in research aimed at exploring African American homeschoolers' identity development and the effects of homeschooling on the transition experiences of first year African American homeschooled college students at PWIs. The past 25 years of research on the academic achievement of home-educated students has consistently shown that the homeschooled students' measure of academic aptitude is equal to those of non-homeschooled students and academically prepared for the rigor of college level curriculum (Belfield, 2005; Bolle et al., 2007; Chatmon, 2006; Clemente, 2006; Kranzow 2005; Qaqish, 2007; Rockney, 2002; White et al. 2007). However, past research has been limited and anecdotal with research subjects predominantly comprised of White homeschoolers. According to Banks (2004), the current public educational system in America is based on the European experience, belief systems, theory, values, and history. Because Eurocentric focused curriculum marginalizes the history and experiences of other ethnic groups, it hinders positive transformative learning and creates barriers that have detrimental effects on how minority groups strive in education.

It is expected that 50% of today's homeschoolers will apply to four-year institutions with an undetermined amount of African American homeschooled applicants (Bielick, 2008; Ray, 2011). While current research has shown that the transition experiences of homeschooled students in general is typical of non-homeschooled students (Bolle et al., 2007; Ray, 2009), the current data is demographically limited on information on the transition experiences of first year African American homeschooled students in particular. Research on the transition of non-homeschooled first year African American college students has identified challenges with social and academic preparedness (Barnett, 2004; Engstrom & Tinto, 2008; Hausmann et al., 2009; Sledge, 2012). Others contended that without the support from family and school instructors, the African American student will not thrive in general (Benner & Mistry, 2007; Feenstra et al, 2009; Herndon, M. & Hirt, J. B. (2004); Stewart, 2006). There is a void in the existing research reviewed aimed at exploring the effects of homeschooling on the transition experiences of African American homeschooled college students at PWIs in comparison to the transition of non-homeschooled African American college students.

With what is already known about specific transitional experiences of non-homeschooled African American college students, and the void in the knowledge base on African American homeschoolers, research on this population was necessary to begin to understand the similarities and differences of how African American homeschoolers transition in comparison to non-homeschooled African American college students.

Estimates by The National Home Education Research Institute and the National Center for Education Statistics, U.S. Department of Education indicate there were approximately 2.5 to 3 million homeschooled K-12 students living in the U.S. in 2012, with an estimated growing population of 222,000 African Americans within the last 5 years (Bielick, 2008). Ray (2011) estimated that 50% of homeschooled children will apply to college. Many college administrators and faculty expressed concerns with the transition of homeschooled students (Jones & Gloeckner, 2004).

Home-based education is now clearly the fastest growing form of education, compared to public and private institutional schooling to date (Ray, 2004b). This rise in homeschooled children has the potential to increase the applications to colleges and universities across the nation, many of which are, and will be increasingly African American, making inquiry into the phenomenon on how this sub-population transition into PWIs necessary.

The literature reviewed in each chapter summarized the pertinent scholarly research on homeschooling, a brief history of the education of Blacks in America, and their challenges transitioning into PWIs. A synthesis of current publications that integrate single studies by scholars and practitioners as a means to research the African American students' college experience in Predominately White Institutions was presented noting the potential challenges that the growing population of African American homeschoolers in college and those preparing to attend college, may experience. The literature review provided a solid foundation for the necessity of the intended research. It has shown a serious gap in the knowledge base and a void in research on African Americans homeschoolers in higher education.

CHAPTER IX
Purpose of the Research Study

The purpose of this study was to explore the transition experiences of homeschooled African Americans into PWIs. With the expected growth of the African American homeschoolers population applying to colleges and universities, higher education should engage in research that explores this emerging population. The research conducted on this subpopulation is useful for college administrators, student affairs practitioners, faculty, and parents of African American homeschooled students to have insight on how these students transition into college in order to be better prepared to address any potential challenges these students may encounter at PWIs. In addition, this research also presents the opportunity to learn about the success of this population, which may inspire or require curriculum, institutional, or policy changes in the future.

With the noted increase of homeschooled African Americans in the United States since 2005 (Ray, 2011), the assumption could be made that an undetermined percentage of those homeschoolers were either now in college, have graduated from college or were applying to college. This chapter presents the findings of the research study to gain insight on two questions:

Purpose of the Research Study

1. What are the transition experiences of Homeschooled African Americans into college and university learning environments of PWIs?
2. How are the transition experiences of African Americans who were homeschooled similar to, or different from, the transition experiences of non-homeschooled African American students at PWIs in higher education?

The questions created for the online questionnaire and live interviews were categorized thematically providing the best insight on the transition experiences of homeschooled African Americans who have attended PWIs in higher education. The 10 categories focused on (a) racial identity, (b) homeschool experience, (c) general campus climate, (d) faculty/administrator perceptions, (e) student perceptions, (f) self-perception; (g) curriculum, (h) social climate, (i) family support, and (j) challenges. Each category played a significant role in transition. This chapter will present the findings for each of the categories in the participants' own words through their lived experiences.

Researchers estimate 50% of homeschoolers will apply to colleges and universities (Bielick, 2008; Egelko & Tucker, 2008; Maxwell & Maxwell, 2008; Ray, 2008, 2011) with an undetermined amount of African American homeschooled applicants (Ray, 2011). Current research conducted by Bolle et al. (2007) and Ray (2009) has shown that the transition experiences of homeschooled students in general are typical of non-homeschooled students transitioning into college. Research on homeschoolers conducted by Kranzow (2005) and White et al. (2007) found that homeschoolers adjust within college social life. However, the research on homeschoolers in college has been limited to the experiences of predominantly White students with data on the experiences of African American homeschooled students who transitioned into college non-existent.

Jones and Gloeckner (2004) stated that although homeschooled students faced stereotypes from faculty, administrators, and peers, they had typical transition experiences similar to non-homeschooled students. According to Ray (2005; 2009) and Van Pelt (2003), homeschooled students had few transition issues and were equally, if not more, academically prepared than non-homeschooled, traditionally educated students. However, it is important to note that the samplings for the limited research that existed focused primarily on the experiences of White homeschooled students.

A plethora of research has been conducted on the transition of first-year African American college students, identifying their challenges as social and academic preparedness (Barnett, 2004; Brown, Morning, & Watkins, 2005; Engstrom & Tinto, 2006; Flowers, 2007; Harvey & Harvey, 2005; Harvey, 2008; Hausman, et al., 2009: Levin et al. 2007; More & Owens, 2008; Sledge, 2012). This study explored the transition experiences of African Americans

Purpose of the Research Study

who were previously homeschooled to learn if transition challenges to those of traditional African American college students are similar. An investigation into this emerging population entering colleges and universities would be an important contribution to the knowledge base.

CHAPTER X

Research Design

A qualitative methodology was chosen as the appropriate method for this research for several reasons: (1) qualitative studies are holistic in nature focusing on the discovery and insight valuing the perspective(s) of the subject being studied while offering some of research's most significant contributions to theory, practice, and policy in the field of education (Creswell, 2007). (2) a phenomenological narrative inquiry approach was utilized to create a descriptive research process based on personally lived experiences. Phenomenology is the study of a phenomenon and how one consciously experiences and makes sense of that phenomenon (Creswell, 1998). (3) It is not uncommon for researchers to utilize a phenomenological approach to focus on the experience of a single individual, or to gather data collected from the individual experiences of a small sample of people to gain a deeper understanding of the experiences because it allows for more depth and breadth to the meaning of lived experiences (Creswell, 2005; van Manen, 1990).

When the social constructs of language merge with the phenomenology of the human experience, it allows for in depth comprehension and qualitative analysis within narrative inquiry that is empirical and valid in research (Casey, 1995-96; Creswell, 2007). This viewpoint of some researchers is due in part to the fact that reliability is a concept that evaluates the quality in quantitative studies, whereas the purpose of the study is exploring to acquire an "understanding" versus "explaining" to answer a problem necessarily (Stenbacka, 2001).

This research design utilized personal interviews focusing on the micro analytic individual stories of formerly homeschooled African Americans who have, or were attending a four-year institution of higher education. This was an informative approach to gain insight on an emerging population through the narrative experiences of the participants.

The sampling for this qualitative study followed the principles of non-probability through a purposive sample. The sampling strategy utilized for the purposive sampling was homogeneous. This method of qualitative research was the most effective because the past 25 years of published research on homeschoolers has been rudimentary, demographically limited, and anecdotal with research subjects being predominantly White homeschoolers. Due to the unknown documented African American homeschoolers who have attended or were now attending a PWI, conducting the study with a homogeneous purposive sampling provided a small window into the personal transition experiences of homeschooled African American college students.

The homogeneous sampling for this qualitative study consisted of participants selected based upon a pre-defined set of criteria: a) participants must have been African American; b) homeschooled from K-12 or during their high school years; c) be 18 - 25 years of age, and have graduated from, currently attending or have attended a PWI as an undergraduate. This purposive sampling consisted of six to twelve participants.

Although the sampling was small, the value of the research was not based on inferences of the general African American homeschooling population. The goal was not to achieve objectivity or to attempt to generalize from the study sample to the wider population of interest, but to explore the intricacies of the sample's transition experiences into PWIs of higher education and set precedence for the inquiry on this under-researched subpopulation.

Qualitative narrative research involves studying the personal experiences of a small sample of participants (Creswell, 2008). According to Patton (2002), there exist no established rules on sample sizes for qualitative research. Small studies continue to contribute significantly to the knowledge base. Piaget's (1972) theory of cognitive development was established based on the qualitative study of his three children. The field of psychoanalysis was established by Freud (Sachs, 1945) based on findings from a sample of less than 10 persons. Bandler & Grinder (1975) founded Neurolinguistic Programming based on studying three subjects. A single case study conducted by Park in 2001 focused on data collected on one individual, the researcher's daughter (Patton, 2002). Numerous dissertations in recent times have been successfully defended by way of qualitative research utilizing samples of one to six participants. The value and validity in phenomenological qualitative studies is that a much deeper exploration of an individual's experience can occur due to the small sample size typical of narrative phenomenological studies (Patton, 2002).

Securing the participants was a challenge due to the limited public information on African American homeschoolers. However, the researcher was able to collect subjects through established homeschool associations and word of mouth communications utilizing the snowball sampling method, a non-probability sampling technique. Snowballing is a research technique utilized when locating participants is difficult (Patton, 2002). The process involves requesting located study participants to refer other potential participants (Patton, 2002). With qualitative non-probability research, different purposive sampling techniques can be utilized individually or in combination with other purposive sampling techniques to assist in the selection process (Yin, 2009).

The researcher utilized publicized homeschool organizations and word of mouth to locate participants. During the recruitment process, the researcher found that African American homeschooling families tend not to be as public as White homeschooling families, although more African American homeschool organizations have emerged over the past 5 years with websites and/or contact information accessible on the Internet, many of the web links were defunct, some of the contacts non-responsive, or Internet groups required an application to join with approval. Many local and national homeschool organizations were contacted during the recruitment effort without regard to the study being race based. This strategy was used in hopes of referrals of African American homeschooling families that may have a son or daughter in college, or one who has attended, or has graduated from college.

There was noted reluctance of African American homeschooling parents and organizations to volunteer to participate in the research study came with a high level of distrust, much of which was revealed during the recruitment effort. Some of these concerns were personally based while others were socially and politically based. With homeschooling laws different from state to state, there were fears held by some of the parents of potential participants of intrusion of state educational agencies that have mandates for homeschooling which might affect the siblings of the potential participant that were still being homeschooled, concerns with legal implications, or that the researcher was merely an informant for law enforcement agencies. There also appeared to be distrust in participation if the researcher did not identify as African American, purpose of the study, and a potential lack of homeschool background. A small Afrocentric homeschool organization expressed their sentiments for declining participation in the research study whose ideology was steeped in anti-White, anti-government dogma. Institutions of higher education, even Historically Black Colleges and Universities, were seen with suspicion by this Afrocentric homeschool organization. Others requested financial compensation for their participation, which could have compromised the research (Creswell, 2008).

The snowballing method of recruiting potential participants was effective in locating male and female participants. Utilizing the snowballing method in conjunction with the researcher's self-disclosure allowed for successful recruitment efforts. I identified as African American researcher with a background in homeschooling provided an environment where the participants felt more comfortable and inclined to participate in the study. As noted by Maxwell (2005), bias and reactivity are two issues that can threaten the validity of qualitative research (Maxwell, 2005).

With my homeschooling background, there were inherent biases that could have threatened the validity of the interpretation of the collected qualitative research data (Merriam, 2002). My identifying as African American with 22 years of involvement in homeschooling could have been a cause for the transfer of bias. However, as Maxwell (2005) stated, it takes the skill of a researcher with good judgment to know when to use a potential influence productively in qualitative research, not to eliminate it.

The goal was to have six to 12 participants of which eight were identified out of 20 potential participants. During the recruitment process, it was noted that many homeschoolers begin colleges younger than 18. One willing participant was a 16-year-old college student who wanted to be a part of the study and the parents were willing to provide consent. An IRB Addendum was submitted for approval to allow the minor's participation. Participants were asked to provide basic demographic information for the researcher's records. The demographics of the research participants were three males and five females. There were three graduates, four freshmen, and one sophomore. Participants were given anonymity to protect their privacy and told that the names of their undergraduate institution attended would not be revealed. Participants attended universities in the states of Virginia, Ohio, and New York, during their undergraduate education. The purposive sample for this study was diverse in age, gender, geographical location, college/university attended, years at college, period of college attendance, homeschool pedagogy, and college discipline.

CHAPTER XI

Analysis of the Findings

Racial Identity

The purposive sampling for this study was homogeneous in that the participants shared common characteristics. One of the characteristics pertinent in exploring the transition experiences of homeschooled African American students into PWIs was to identify as and be African American as defined by the operational definition of terms for this study. Since "race" has been noted as playing an integral role in personal development, as well as how the racial dynamics of PWIs directly influence the transition and persistence of African American college students (Adams, 2005; Anglin & Wade, 2007; Herndon & Hirt, 2004), participants were asked how they identify racially. While all the participants identify as "Black" or "African American" several participants were also very aware of other races in their bloodline. Several of the participants noted that although they may possess physical attributes from their ancestral bloodline that might confuse an onlooker as to which racial group they belong to, they were not confused, and they identified as African American because that is their experience in the social setting of America.

Analysis of the Findings

Dialogue during the interview process revealed that participants were cognizant of race at a young age. Three of the participants indicated that talk of race relations was a common discussion topic within their immediate households as well as in the households of their extended family. "...I remember hearing the adults' discussions and debates on race..." another participant stated, "...you just knew who you were...there was no question in my house...there was an understanding before you could even walk or talk..." Most participants appeared to be conscious of the concept of race and their racial identity as young children.

There were a few participants who stated that they were sometimes confused for other races such as Jewish, Jamaican, Latino, Asian, or biracial. It is possible that this may have played a role in their transition experience to a certain degree if their race is not made known. Participant #2 stated that he was never conscious of his race, never felt singled out, or discriminated because of his race, nor had he experienced any challenges due to his race.

It was clear from the interviews of participants who were sometimes confused for other races; at some point during their transition experience how they racially identified was made known. Skin tone bias was experienced by Participants #5 and #6 who noticed the difference in treatment by of some White students who assumed they were of another race when they learned she identified as African American. Participants #5 and #6 also noticed how African American students reacted towards them, assuming they were not African American. Both reactions would be negative. However, even after some African Americans learned that Participants #5 and #6 identified as African American there was still a feeling of negativity. Interestingly enough, these participants would note that negativity was felt from both dark and light-skinned African Americans. Participant #6 attributed the negativity from light skinned African Americans to her hair being in an ethnic hairstyle sometimes referred to as "dreadlocks," she would attribute the negativity from dark skinned African Americans to her being fair skinned with long hair. What was significant about the responses to racial identity was that none of the participants noted these as challenges, albeit negative, had somewhat of an impact on their socialization, but did not pose an impasse to their academic achievement. This was consistent with the research by scholars Adams, (2005); Anglin & Wade, (2007); Herndon & Hirt, (2004); Smith, & Hopkins, (2004) who have a consensus that African American students who have a knowledge base of their own history, identify and embrace their culture maneuver within the culture of PWIs with less difficulty academically and socially than those lacking in this development.

Although tangential to the purpose of this research, outlier themes arose within this category among the female participants on the subject of same race discrimination due to skin tone, hair texture, and length. Participants #5 and #8 shared similar sentiments. A qualitative research study conducted to better understand the challenges of African American students attending a PWI by Fries-Britt and Turner (2001) with 15 African American participants established three themes: Racial stereotypes; Race-based insults on physical characteristics; and challenges to their intellectual competence. These themes were experienced by African American students from their White peers. The purpose of this study was to explore the college transition experiences of homeschooled African Americans students at PWIs yet the participants of this study claim to have experienced more Racial stereotypes; Race-based insults on physical characteristics; and challenges to their intellectual competence from their African American peers even more so than their White peers. This finding deviated from the established literature on the transition experience of African American students at PWIs.

The experience of racial bias perpetrated by African Americans towards each other came as a surprise to the study participants and is an outlier theme within the research due to the focus of the purpose of this study. While these participants did not suggest that these experiences affected them academically, it is possible this could still be seen as a potential challenge as it is consistent with "stereotype threat" as defined by researcher Steele (1997, 2010).

The results of the longitudinal quantitative study conducted by researchers Nasim et al., (2005) to investigate how race impacted the way African Americans achieved in PWIs, indicated that racial identity significantly impacted their academic performance while attending these colleges and universities. However, these results were not necessarily consistent with how race impacted homeschooled African American college students. None of the participants, while aware of the dynamics of race and the role it plays at PWIs, expressed that their racial experiences with White or African American students hindered their academic success or how they transitioned. In fact, this finding deviated from the response patterns of African American college students noted in the existing research on the transition experiences of African American college students at PWIs (Anglin & Wade, 2007; Brown et al., 2005; Cross, 1991; Grant-Vallone et al., 2004; Karemera et al., 2003; Kim, 2007; Kuh & Hu, 2001; McDonald & Vrana, 2007; Nasim et al., 2005; Nicpon et al., 2006, 2007; Parker & Flowers, 2003).

All of the participants appeared to hold critical thinking skills that allowed them to process their racial experiences, both negative and positive, and act upon them in a manner that did not allow the negative experiences to impede upon their educational goals. The level of awareness, consciousness, comfort, and pride the participants already possessed and expressed coming into college in regard to their racial identity and the issue of being African American in a PWI may have played a significant role in why their racial identity did not prove to be a challenge in their transition into higher education. More in depth dialogue in regards to why their racial identity did not present a challenge in their academic achievement could use further investigation. Under the category of "racial identity," interview questions could use some revision to stay in line with the purpose of the study. For example, question number seven: "What role does knowing the history of your race play in your life?" This question may have presented more in depth responses more in line with the purpose of the research study if rephrased, "Does studying the history of one's own race play any significant role in education? If so how? If not, why not?"

Homeschool Experience

Duggan (2010), Goodman (2008), and Lisle (2006) have all found that research on the homeschooled student showed that the success of homeschoolers in college is in part due to their homeschool educational background. In order to gain insight on how homeschooled African Americans transition into PWIs of higher education, it is necessary to learn about the pre-college education of the participants. Examining the home school educational backgrounds of the participants will show how their compulsory education impacted their college transition experience.

According to Ray (2004b), homeschooled students are independently motivated, accustomed to highly individualized, flexible learning programs and self-directed learning opportunities typically developed or implemented by parents. Although less than half of the participants shared that their homeschool education had set curriculum at least during their primary years, the majority stated that their homeschool curriculum was individualized, flexible, and eventually self-directed during their last years of homeschool education. This would be consistent with the results of Ray's (2004b) research study on homeschoolers.

Opponents of homeschooling (Apple, 2006; Hudak, 2003; Lubienski, 2003; Reich, 2002) questioned the homeschool curriculum with concern of randomness and lack of compatibility to that of public school education. There were also concerns by homeschool opponents of curriculum being steeped in religious beliefs limiting the cultural and intellectual diversity of learning. However, several of the participants experienced a set curriculum that was standardized and similar to public school.

Homeschool opponents concern of the lack of cultural diversity was not present with the participants of this study who all stated that their homeschool learning experience was multicultural or had a multicultural component. Participant #8 shared that the home décor consisted of huge world maps, artifacts from around the world, globes, and international movies and world music. Participants studied foreign languages as well as participated in international festivals. Some of the participants lived and traveled out of the country and experienced international cities. Some participants were dual enrolled or attended community colleges before applying to four-year institutions while others applied directly to four-year institutions, consistent with the research of Bolle et al., (2007); Kranzow, (2005); and White et al. (2007).

Bowditch (2003) questioned the lack of socialization of homeschoolers due to overprotective parents. As noted in Chapter IV, participants described the setting where most of their education took place as within their homes, supplemented with outside activities and extracurricular activities within and outside their communities such as competitive sports, art classes, African dance, ballet, and music lessons. Participant #3 was an accomplished violinist upon entering college, two others performed in an orchestra; Participant #8 is a classical pianist and plays African drums for an African Dance Company. Most participated in summer camp activities held at universities in the STEM fields and English/Writing. They spoke of field trips and multicultural activities.

All the participants shared a positive consensus that most significant aspect of their homeschool learning experience was the freedom to learn at their own pace, freedom to explore and guide their own curriculum, flexibility to set their own schedules, culturally diverse curriculum, and no peer pressure/bullying. This consensus was consistent with surveys conducted by Ray (2003, 2004a, 2004b, and 2005) with homeschooling parents, which listed poor curriculum, bullying at public schools and flexibility in learning at home as their reasons for homeschooling their children.

A single research study conducted by Fields-Smith and Williams, published in the *Urban Review* in 2009, is currently one of only two published research studies available on African American homeschoolers. The Fields-Smith and Williams (2009) study focused on African American parents' motivations that attributed to their decision to homeschool their children. What the research would find is that one of the most noted reasons why African American parents decided to homeschool their children was the lack of cultural sensitivity and Eurocentric centered curriculum. Participants #5, #6, and #8 shared that they had learning material that reflected their likeness from children's books to Black and African histories and that their parents saw it important that they had this foundation even before learning Western civilization and the histories of other cultures as young children.

A consistent theme found in investigating participants' home school education, was that their mothers were their primary instructors. This phenomenon is an excellent topic for future research and possibly as a comparative study between races. Another theme was that during the last few years of participants' compulsory education, it became self-directed with their mothers, acting as guides. The self-directedness of learning was viewed as one of the best parts about being homeschooled and consistent with the research of Ray (2004b). Participants also acknowledged that although the freedom of self-directed learning was available to them that, they were still required to produce schoolwork in a timely manner.

However, what was inconsistent with Ray's (2004b) research results in comparison with the participants of this study is that Ray (2004b) claimed home schooling parents put greater academic emphasis on learning rather than testing. Some parents of homeschooled African Americans participating in this study utilized online curriculum as well as academic software to enhance their child's education; as well as standardized testing to evaluate academic progress.

This would refute, in part, the sweeping claim of Rothermel (2003) that homeschool curriculums lacked oversight or comparable course work compared to standard public school curriculum that better prepared the student for college. This also refutes Reich's (2005) concerns with homeschools adhering to curriculum standards, but participants of this study stated that there needs to be a balance in the study of basic disciplines such as college math and Western Civilization. A common theme expressed was challenges with Eurocentric centered curriculum.

While issues with math were not reflected in the outcomes of the research on homeschoolers transition into college conducted on predominantly White students, math appeared to be a weak area with some of the African American homeschoolers for yet unexplored reasons. The challenges of college level history courses were noted by participants as being too Eurocentric. Most the participants of this research received a multicultural-based history education from an African American perspective.

Noted patterns in this category were that most participants were homeschooled from K-12 and went from homeschool directly into four-year PWIs. Another noted pattern was that participants' learning became more "self-directed" once they began or were in secondary education. Most notable was the fact that every participant's mother held the leading role as primary instructor.

Additional data is needed in this category. More background information on the participants' parents would have been useful. A recently published dissertation by Sherman (2012) on a small qualitative case study and a small qualitative study with a phenomenological approach conducted by Fields-Smith & Williams (2009) provided insight on why African American parents decided to homeschool their children. This exploratory study would have benefited from interviewing the participants' parents as well. Areas to explore by interviewing the parents of homeschooled African American students now attending college would be: parent/s decision to homeschool; parent/s education background; teaching philosophy; teaching style; educational resources; choice of text books; curriculum development; as well as student assessments and evaluations. Information in these categories and how they chose the college their son or daughter attends will significantly contribute to understanding how homeschooled African American college students transition.

General Campus Climate

All of the participants stated that the college/university they are attending, or did attend, had a friendly, inclusive atmosphere overall. A qualitative research study held by Holder (2001) and qualitative research study conducted by Bolle et al. (2007) both reported that homeschoolers adjust to college environments no differently than non-homeschoolers and that first year homeschoolers experienced similar common transition experiences as non-homeschooled college students such as loneliness, independence, and making new friends. The findings of the current study provided information by the participants consistent with the results of the research studies of Holder (2001) and Bolle et al. (2007).

Based on research by Bolle et al. (2007), Jones and Gloeckner (2004), and Tinto (1982, 1993), socialization would be one of the challenges of homeschoolers. A qualitative study of six previously homeschooled college students by Bolle et al. (2007) attending a Midwestern college in the U.S., focused on the transition of the study participants first year showed that homeschoolers experienced similar common transition experiences as non-homeschooled college students such as loneliness, independence and making new friends. Participant #6 attributed socializing challenges to being introverted and living in a rural community. However, three other participants in the current study were also raised in rural communities and did not have the same issues. Another participant also claimed being an introvert as a challenge with socializing.

Considering the research conducted by Jones and Gloeckner (2004) and Tinto (1982, 1993), it is not certain in the current study whether becoming acclimated to the campus climate for homeschooled African Americans was typical of White homeschoolers or non-homeschooled students. Participants were questioned about the college atmosphere at the institution they attended and services for homeschoolers. While participants claimed they did not experience any unusual transitioning, it was noted that support systems for "homeschoolers" were non-existent. Participants were divided on the necessity of such support. All of the participants stated that the college/university they are attending, or did attend, had a friendly, inclusive atmosphere overall.

However, when participants were asked if their experiences at college had any similarities or differences than non-African American homeschooled students, or if their experience at college had any similarities or differences than other African American students, the responses were mixed and did not necessarily coincide with the current research on the transition experiences of homeschoolers or

African American college students. When asked if their experience at college was similar or different than non- African American homeschoolers, responses were inconsistent as there were a few who saw their transition experience no different from other homeschoolers into higher education. Albeit, most of the participants were not aware of other homeschoolers at their institution to actually do a comparison during the time they attended as freshmen, but most knew of someone within their community that was formerly homeschooled and now attending college, or became aware of others as they became upper classmen which was utilized as a gauge. The majority of the participants' inference that their transition into higher education was not similar to White homeschoolers' challenges as indicated in past research conducted by Ray (2000b, 2001, 2005, and 2009) and Van Pelt (2003), which proclaimed no uncommon transition experiences of homeschoolers transitioning into higher education than those of their peers. Race or gender was not a consideration.

    Participants reflected upon the comparison of their transition experience with that of other African Americans, and while acknowledging the commonality of being of the same race and sharing the Black experience within a societal context, participants did not all assert that their transition experience was exactly the same as other African American students at college due to being homeschooled and not having had experienced public school socialization. Studies on the transition, retention, and matriculation of

African American students document the interview and survey responses from participating students on their experience and stressors at PWIs. These stressors were isolation, professor bias, biased grading practices, financial, racism from White administrators, faculty and students; lack of African American professors, being accused by peers of "acting White," discriminatory institutional policies as well as White advisors and counselors who did not understand their experience (Anglin & Wade, 2007; Antonio et al., 2005; Chang & Demyan, 2007; Flowers, 2007; Greer & Chwalisz, 2007; Harvey & Harvey, 2005; Harvey, 2008; Levin et al., 2007; Moore & Owens, 2008; Reid & Radhakrishnan, 2003; Negga, et al., 2007; Smith & Hopkins, 2004).

Information collected from participants of this study did not refute that challenges do not exist for African Americans at PWIs. In fact, several participants cited some of the exact stressors identified by the plethora of research studies conducted on the transition experiences of African Americans into PWIs. However, these stressors were not cited by the participants as challenges that impeded upon their academic success or their social or cultural capital in the context of education. Some of the participants stated that they saw themselves taking their education more seriously than some of the other African Americans that were struggling. A few others simply felt they responded to the challenges preset at PWIs differently than some of the other African Americans who were struggling with race relations, scholastics, and study habits.

Cuyjet (2006b) found that African American males have one of the highest failure rates in academic success, transition, and retention issues. Other scholars in the field supported Cuyjet's (2006b) findings regarding the challenges of African American males in PWIs such as having the tendency to require more than four years to matriculate; being not academically prepared for college level course work; lacking good study skills; and not engaging in college activities that are purposeful educationally or deemed to be necessary in order to acquire a certain level of social capital for more simplified transitioning and collegiate navigation (Bonner & Bailey, 2006; Cruce et al., 2006; Harper, 2006; Kuh & Hu, 2001; Nelson Laird, et al., 2007; Palmer & Hilton, 2008; Strayhorn, 2008). This would not be the case for the homeschooled African Americans male participants of this study, some of whom viewed their experience as similar to other African American men due to their shared experience in many regards, but also different due to observing how some African Americans were less focused on academic achievement and excelling and more focused on socializing. Another participant saw his experience differently from African American students that were public school or private school educated due to having developed time management skills and prioritizing tasks while being homeschooled that transferred over into college life. Other participants saw their experience differently than that of African American students based on what they saw as the lack of acceptance of one's own culture or interest in socializing with students of all cultures.

Overall, the participants of this exploratory research would transition into the general campus climate holding certain commonalities with both homeschooled African American college students and formerly homeschooled college students. Aspects of their experiences were reflective in previous research studies, observations, perceptions, and the research cited on how homeschooled and African American college students respond to stressors unique to being homeschoolers and African Americans. However, challenges becoming acclimated were noted as not appearing to create barriers to the academic success or retention of homeschooled African American college students of this study.

The lack of a common theme among all the participants in the category of "General Campus Climate" identified that male participants became acclimated to the general campus climate with more ease than the female participants. More research is necessary to determine if homeschooled African American females transition differently into college than homeschooled African American males.

Analysis of the Findings

Faculty/Administrator Perceptions

Research on homeschoolers conducted by Jones and Gloeckner (2004) discovered that college and university admission officers across the United States continued to grapple with how to address a growing population of newly graduated home schooled students each year. They also affirmed that negative perceptions on behalf of college administrators, teachers, counselors, and even some college students as the biggest transition obstacles homeschoolers face. As noted in the literature review, studies on the transition, retention, and matriculation of African American students document some of the stressors at PWIs as professor bias, biased grading practices, racism from White administrators and faculty, lack of African American professors as well as White advisors and counselors who did not understand their experience (Anglin & Wade, 2007; Antonio et al., 2005; Chang & Demyan, 2007; Flowers, 2007; Grant-Vallone, Reid, Umali, & Pohlert, 2003, 2004; Moore & Owens, 2008; Reid & Radhakrishnan, 2003).

While most of the participants felt that they were fairly treated by faculty and administrators and that their professors eventually saw them as serious students, Participant #5 had a mixed experience. Participant #5 had challenges with some faculty, administrators and her advisor due to their knowledge of her incoming homeschooled status. Several noted that not all of their professors were aware of their incoming status as "homeschooled." Others stated that it was not clear if their negative experiences with faculty and administrators were due solely to being "homeschooled," being African American, both, or neither. One participant felt some of the negativity included signs of gender bias.

According to Gay (2000), contributions to the class by students not of the dominant culture were not as valued as White students, many times their work was graded highly critically, and unfairly with feedback that is negative, discouraging, destructive and even demeaning. Several participants indicated issues they had with bad advisors and faculty whose grading practices in regard to them were questionable. Each made a point to meet with their faculty and to obtain clarity on and justification for their grades. Participant #5 observed that other African American students merely complained to other students or were happy with a hard "C" instead of making an appointment to meet with their professor for clarity or an opportunity to improve the grade.

A noted pattern was participants stated that they made it a point to meet with their advisors, sought tutoring if necessary, and/or were part of study groups. It is important to note that they would find themselves as the lone African American at some of the study groups or extra credit workshops. This emerging theme could be an impetus for an investigation on how African American students respond to grades they are not satisfied with receiving.

Although participants of this study cited challenges at some point in their college education with faculty and administrators, most expressed that they felt they were seen as serious students and treated fairly. Another pattern identified was that participants made it a point to meet with their professors during professor office hours to share their concerns, as well as their ideas and interest in the coursework. However, participants did not state their challenges created an impasse or that they did not possess the skill set capacity to maneuver through successfully. The findings in this subcategory of faculty/administrator perceptions would not be consistent in its entirety with the research conducted by Jones & Gloeckner (2004). In fact, the issues of neither race nor gender were taken into account in their study. Consideration should also be taken in regards to the faculty and administrative culture at the individual institutions that may vary from one college to the next depending upon how progressive each may be. Other points to consider are how many homeschoolers apply and attend, as well as the diversity of those incoming homeschoolers.

Student Perceptions

A qualitative study on the racial dynamics on PWI campuses as experienced by African American students was conducted by

Solorzano (2000). Information gathered from the participants of Solorzano's study expressed being stereotyped negatively regarding their academic propensity by White students with racial tensions in and outside the classroom, as well as feelings of segregation, all of which significantly affected their self-esteem and academic performance. Another qualitative research study conducted to understand the challenges of African American students attending a PWI better by Fries-Britt & Turner (2001) established three themes: Racial stereotypes, race-based insults on physical characteristics, and challenges to their intellectual competence.

Participants of this study were asked to share how they were treated by African American students, White students, other racial groups, as well as other homeschoolers. All responded as to not having any serious problems with the international student body. Most felt that they were seen as a serious student and their contributions to their classes valued in general.

However, the research studies of Solorzano (2000) and Fries-Britt & Turner (2001) would not be entirely consistent with the previously homeschooled African American college students of this research study, many of whom expressed experiencing the racial and stereotypical overtones of being homeschooled and African American by both Black and White students. However, none expressed these experiences affecting their self-esteem or their academic performance.

Research conducted on environmental perceptions of PWIs by Phillips (2005) compared the perceptions of White and African

American students at a predominantly White campus revealed that African Americans students felt marginalized causing them to experience academic difficulty and socialization issues. According to Phillips (2005), these feelings of marginalization seriously impacted the retention rates of African Americans. Several of the participants voiced how their White peers did not expect to be outperformed by African American students. Their White peers would become attitudinal when they found that they were not as academically prepared as an African American student. None of the participants of this study expressed any feelings of being marginalized by the perceptions of White students. Participants #5 & #6 expressed perceptions of African American peers as trying to be White, equating intelligence and worldliness as characteristics only attributed to White students.

    This was a common theme among several of the participants accused of "acting White" by their African American peers because of their knowledge base. These examples could be seen as forms of "stereotype threat" as defined by Steele & Aronson (1995) in their studies on "stereotyping" and how African American students internalize beliefs of inferiority to Whites in the area of intellect. However, in this study, the internalization beliefs of inferiority to Whites in the area of intellect would be held by both White and African American students towards homeschooled African American college students. Experiencing same race stereotyping would resonate with the participants significantly. Conducting interviews with faculty and administrators from each of the participants' institution on their perceptions and attitudes of African American homeschoolers could have provided more insight for this category on the phenomena of how homeschooled African American students transition into PWIs of higher education.

Self-Perception

All of the participants in this research study saw themselves as highly confident as well as having a broad based homeschool learning experience. Although two participants admitted to already being introverts and not "fitting in" as easily at their college, none had feelings of marginalization at the institutions they attended or that it dramatically impacted them academically or socially. Although they saw themselves as having some similarities with other African American college students, they also saw strong differences in how they were socialized, academically prepared, their political and global views, as well as how they approached solving problem. As the semesters moved forward, students would eventually find their niche of friends.

All of the participants saw themselves as studious, focused, with academic goals, and a plan on how they were going to achieve them. Most saw themselves as equally if not more intelligent than the average college student and academically prepared for the rigors of higher education. This would reflect the research of Ray (2009), and Van Pelt, (2003) who professed that homeschooled students were equally, if not more, academically prepared than non-homeschooled traditionally educated students. Patterns identified in this category were time management and study habits which participants attributed to their academic success. A common theme was prioritizing, staying focused, and having academic goals to achieve.

Curriculum

The past 25 years of research on the academic achievement of home educated students has consistently shown that the homeschooled students' measure of academic aptitude is equal to, if not higher than, those of non-homeschooled students, making them academically prepared for the rigor of a college level curriculum (Belfield, 2005; Bolle et al., 2007; Chatmon, 2006; Clemente, 2006; Kranzow 2005; Qaqish, 2007; Rockney, 2002; White et al., 2007). This study explored a plethora of research on the transition of non-homeschooled first year African American college students which identified challenges with social and academic preparedness (Barnett, 2004; Brown, Morning, & Watkins, 2005; Engstrom, & Tinto, 2008; Hausmann et al., 2009; Sledge, 2012).

According to Gay (2002), students from non-dominant groups at PWIs were struggling to strive in a learning environment that continued to utilize mainstream hidden curriculum, further alienating them from their own cultural contributions and experiences within the dominant culture. Their contributions to the class were typically seen as not as valued as White students. Many times their work was graded more critically and unfairly, with feedback that was negative, discouraging, destructive, and even demeaning. Banks (2004) articulated that Eurocentric focused curriculum marginalized the history and experiences of other ethnic groups; it hindered positive transformative learning and created barriers, which had detrimental effects on how minority groups strived in education.

All of the participants contributed their academic success to being focused, having good study habits and being confident. Most believed their homeschooling academically prepared them for college. However, some participants admitted to challenges with math and history. What has been recognized about the general characteristics of homeschoolers is that they are accustomed to diverse and dynamic learning environments where they receive one-on-one attention and self-directed learning opportunities (Ray, 2004b). Compared with most students educated conventionally, Ray (2004b) believed homeschooling parents put greater academic emphasis on learning rather than testing. Ray (2004b) also proclaimed that homeschooled students were independently motivated and accustomed to highly individualized and flexible learning programs that are typically developed or implemented by college-educated parents. What Ray (2004b) espoused is constant with the experiences of the participants of this study.

Participants #4, #5, and #6 shared their struggles with college level math, as well. More research is needed to understand why this may be the case among African American homeschoolers. It may be hypothesized that homeschooling African American parents may possibly have a math deficit. However, all of the participants of this study came from homes where one if not both parents held college degrees with a few even holding advanced graduate and terminal degrees. Participants that followed a more standardized curriculum experienced less difficulty with freshman required core curriculum. This research found that some of the participants that did not follow a standardized curriculum struggled in some disciplines, such as math. If this was found legitimate, it would support Rothermel (2003) who claimed that homeschool curriculum lacked comparable course work to standard public school curriculum, not preparing the student for the rigor of college coursework.

The challenges with history reflect Banks' (2004) concerns that Eurocentric focused curriculum marginalized the history and experiences of other ethnic groups. The participants who experienced challenges with college history courses were not due to a deficit in their knowledge base, but more that of frustration with receiving history instruction based on the Eurocentric perspective.

Several participants admitted there was a non-Eurocentric approach to history during their homeschooling even when it came to Western Civilization. This approach may have played a role in the challenges that some participants experienced in their college history course work. Some frequently found themselves in hot debates on the facts of historical events or that their race's historical events were simply dismissed or inaccurate, also consistent with Banks' (2004) concerns that Eurocentric focused curriculum marginalized the history and experiences of other ethnic groups.

These sentiments would also be felt regarding other course work besides history by Participant #5, who attended a Christian-based university where the focus was Western Civilization.

Participant #6 saw a status quo mindset behind the curriculum during her time at her university. The curriculum was seen as a tool to groom and homogenize students, which is a form of socialization to prepare students for life in America within the constraints of the dominant society. Brint (2005) discussed "moral conformity" as a form of training through compulsory education that consists of character building that understands, internalizes and produces actions that are in line with the belief system, ethics, virtues, and values of the dominant culture. Participant #5 insinuated that a kind of hidden curriculum possibly exists in higher education, as well.

Participants of this study saw that their college curriculum had the typical challenges of Eurocentric dominance and the general challenges of college course work to all students. However, although participants of this study pinpointed academic challenges that they faced, of which many were similar challenges African American college students identified through empirical research conducted by scholars in the field such as Eurocentric centered curriculum and academic challenges (Antonio et al., 2005; Flowers, 2007; Harvey, 2008; Levin et al., 2007; Moore & Owens, 2008), none saw these challenges as having any detrimental effects on how they strived academically.

Participants shared how they sought tutoring and joined study groups; met with advisors and faculty to address issues with grades, course work or degree track. Most of the participants expressed that overall their contributions to class discussions were valued by both faculty and students. Common themes for this category were concerns with Eurocentric based curriculum, the amount of course work covered in a specified time, and being opinionated on subject matters.

Social Climate

Socialization is the process of becoming competent in the ways of behaving within the dominant culture's social norms and standards through enculturation that is passed down from one generation to the next (Brint, 2006). Socialization in education trains students in the social norms that are expected of them as students within a controlled learning environment that attempts to develop acceptable characteristics and behaviors that will be internalized and transferred outside of the classroom into their communities, employment, and the society at large (Brint, 2006).

Research studies that focused on the transition of First Year homeschoolers would show that homeschoolers experienced similar common transition experiences as non-homeschooled college students such as loneliness, independence, and making new friends, but adjust well within the college social life (Bolle et al., 2007; Kranzow, 2005; White et al. 2007). However, research on the transition of non-homeschooled first year African American college students has identified challenges with social preparedness (Barnett, 2004; Engstrom, & Tinto, 2008; Hausmann et al., 2009; Sledge, 2012).

All of the participants of this study stated that they believed they were socially prepared for college attributing it to being self-confident, socially aware, and having a culturally diverse world perspective with experience. Participants experienced a common transition just as the average college student which would support research conducted by Bolle et al. (2007); Kranzow (2005), and White (2007). The dynamics of ethnicity and social identity on college campuses can affect how students transition as well as have negative effects on students personally and academically (Sidanius et al., 2004). Consistent with the current research, several participants expressed that socializing with other African Americans as the most challenging. These former homeschoolers were not expecting such same race bias and prejudices at the university level among African American students.

However, unlike the results of empirical research on the transition experiences of African Americans who struggle with racial tensions that interfere with and complicate their transition into PWIs, the participants of this study were not dramatically affected when faced with these challenges where it impacted and compromised their scholastics and ability to matriculate. Participants arrived at college confident, racially identified, comfortable as well as racially and culturally aware.

Participants engaged in college activities, sports, and were all able to develop suitable friendships with all types of students from multiple cultures, races and genders. Participants were able to identify cliques as well as the racist, prejudiced people, and bigots within the mesosystem of their attended colleges and universities early on in their transition. Participants of the study appeared to be able to have new experiences, not all of which were positive yet were able to manage to maneuver successfully without these experiences affecting their grades or their desire to continue with their academic studies.

Defying one of the stereotypes of homeschoolers lacking social skills, these participants appeared to be particularly socially aware which could be attributed to how they were homeschooled.

While noting the challenges of socializing at a PWI, these participants attributed their confidence in themselves as the reason why these social challenges did not pose a threat to their transition or their academic achievement. Even two of the participants who saw themselves as introverts still considered themselves confident people and students. Perhaps this confidence could be attributed to something the participants may have gained within the dynamics of their home environment and learned from their homeschooling, in addition to family support. More research in this area would be required to identify the source of confidence in African American homeschooled students. The information gathered for this category is consistent with the research of scholars Adams, (2005); Anglin & Wade, (2007); Herndon & Hirt, (2004); Smith, & Hopkins, (2004) who assert that African American college students who have a sense of their own history and culture tend to transition into PWIs with less difficulty.

Family Support

Family played a central role in the participants' lives during their homeschool education and continued through their college education. While all the participants identified their mother as their primary instructor, many of their fathers acted in the supportive role in charge of certain activities at times, as an advisor and study partner/tutor other times. Many of the participants came from large or

Analysis of the Findings

extended families that played a role as a support system even if just emotionally.

Unlike Tinto's theory (1982, 1993) on how incoming freshman college students transition successfully into higher education socially and academically, where Tinto avowed that the student will experience three distinct stages during their transition of separation from their family and community to acquiring new norms and values than that of their past, family and community support were valued by all the participants and seen as important factors in college student success, some participants discussed having members of their community in support of their education from homeschool through college. One participant shared that even her local mailperson was supportive, the director of their community social service organization, their local librarian, as well as the local newspapers that followed her homeschool educational journey all the way into college. Many had the support of extended family and their church congregations.

Although many participants admitted, enjoying their newly found independence, a pattern was noted, that many made it a point to come home often because it provided the opportunity to regroup from the hustle of college life and classes, as well as for academic advice and emotional support. There was a consensus on the importance of family support. This finding would be consistent with the research of Feenstra, (2001); Stewart, (2006); and Benner & Mistry, (2007) who found that without the support from family and school instructors, the African American student would not thrive in general.

Since homeschooling is a deliberate choice of parents which directly engages parents in all aspects of their child's academic success (Ray, 2001) such continued engagement and support with their child's educational journey would attribute to why participants of this study have transitioned without incident and have been and continue to be successful academically. The bond that participants already possessed with their parents coupled with being their scholastic instructor, advisor, and advocate for academic success throughout their homeschool education was continuous throughout their college education, as well.

The importance of parental support has been documented by scholars in the field of education for all levels of education in order to ensure academic success and student retention (Herndon & Hirt, 2004). Historically, African American families have utilized extended family for support and direction (Herndon & Hirt, 2004). From the information gathered in the current research, homeschooled African American parents are immersed in their child's education as their child's primary educators. The shared confidences among the participants, their determination to be academically successful, as well as their coping skills were attributed in part to family support. Longitudinal studies on African American homeschoolers with kindergarten to undergraduate completion would shed more insight regarding student support systems.

Analysis of the Findings

Challenges

Studies on the transition, retention, and matriculation of African American students in the literature review of this research study documents responses from participating students on their experience and stressors at PWIs. Some the challenges identified were: professor bias, biased grading practices, racism from White administrators, faculty and students; lack of African American professors, being accused by peers of "acting White," discriminatory institutional policies, as well as White advisors and counselors who did not understand their experience.

Participants of this study expressed similar stressors and challenges of transitioning into college as former homeschoolers and African Americans both socially and academically. While there were aspects of the participants' transition experiences typical of all incoming freshmen to any college, there were also thematic commonalities in the challenges of the participants unique to their experience as previously homeschooled African Americans.

Participant #2 expressed challenges with breaking through negative stereotypes associated with being homeschooled as well as issues with White students. Participant #6 also shared her struggles adjusting socially, making friends, separation from her siblings, and the importance of continued support from family.

Participants #6 and #8 expressed concerns with homeschool curriculum being relative to what will be expected knowledge when they arrive at college. While participants with more unstructured, self-directed homeschool experiences appreciated their academic freedom, they saw discrepancies in how coursework from certain disciplines were taught as well as some college math challenges. Challenges with college math were an issue for less than half of the participants. This challenge could be attributed to the level of college math being challenging to most students, or that higher levels of math are not as much as a priority as basic college level math. Participant #5 saw foreign language as a necessary component in homeschooling.

Several participants noted the lack of African American and minority faculty and administrators which gave the impression that not only were they attending a PWI, they were attending a college that did not value diversity or multicultural curriculum. Participants saw the deficiency of diverse faculty and administrators as a potential challenge. The importance of variety of perspectives was also noted by the participants as well as how imperative it is that students experience this from a diverse faculty, student body, as well as multicultural curriculum. Participants racially and socially aware, as well as exposed to multiple cultures appeared to be better prepared them to cope with expected discrimination and inequities encountered at the PWI they attended.

While there were common themes for this category, there were some inconsistencies with what was perceived as a "challenge" although not seen as a "challenge" affecting the transition of the participants. There was a sense that noted challenges by the participants were viewed as simply challenges, expected and unexpected, they were already prepared to deal with or possessed the coping, critical thinking, and problem solving skills to address.

CHAPTER XII

Conclusion

The last 25 years of research on the academic achievements of home educated students held locally, statewide, and now nationally, has consistently shown that the homeschooled students' measure of academic aptitude is equal to, if not higher than, those of non-homeschooled students. Based on these findings, researchers proclaimed homeschoolers were academically prepared for the rigors of a college level curriculum (Belfield, 2005; Bolle et al., 2007; Chatmon, 2006; Clemente, 2006; Kranzow, 2005; Qaqish, 2007; Rockney, 2002; White et al., 2007).

The past research has been rudimentary, demographically limited, and anecdotal with research subjects being predominantly White homeschoolers (Nemer, 2000). The purpose of the study was to explore the transition experiences of homeschooled African Americans into PWIs. This research study has attempted to answer the following questions:

1. *What are the transition experiences of homeschooled African Americans into college and university learning environments of Predominately White Institutions?*

The transition experience of homeschooled African Americans into college and university learning environments of Predominately

Conclusion

White Institutions consisted of some typical transitional experiences common to most college students learning the culture of a new environment, such as becoming acclimated to faculty, administration and the student body, making new friends, and adjusting to the college course load. Homeschooled African American college students experience academic biases from both African American and White students, as well as by some faculty, and challenges because of the limited multicultural scope of the college curriculum and the diversity of the faculty and administration.

Homeschooled African American college students experienced same race challenges from other African American students such as not having the same cultural socialization, being more culturally aware and academically advanced than many, seen as different, arrogant, "acting White" or not "Black" enough. In addition to these challenges, homeschooled African American college students may struggle with some college curriculum if their homeschool curriculum was not equivalent to the standard curriculum of public school education or if their homeschool curriculum was religious, political, Afrocentric, or multicultural based.

2. *How are the transition experiences of African Americans who were homeschooled similar to or different from the transition experiences of non- homeschooled African American students at PWIs in higher education?*

This research study found that the transition experiences of African Americans who were homeschooled are only similar to the transition experiences of non-homeschooled African American students at PWIs in higher education. Because these students share the commonality of the African American experience, they are faced with similar challenges as identified by established empirical research on the experience of African American college students attending PWIs.

This research study also found that the transition experiences of homeschooled African Americans are different from the transition experiences of non-homeschooled African American students because although faced with the same challenges as non-homeschooled African Americans, academic and matriculation outcomes were not consistent with those of non-homeschooled African Americans. Braxton, Hirschy, & McClendon (2004) averred that student entry characteristics play a significant role on their transition and retention in college. The ability to adapt in a new environment is also contingent upon acquired contextual knowledge that can help provide a systemic understanding of an institution's climate (Bean & Eaton, 2000; Conley, 2007). According to Constantine, Wilton, and Caldwell, (2003), African Americans utilize different coping styles in reaction to stressors. Homeschooled African American students in this study appeared to transition into higher education with cognitive strategies as well as meta-cognitive and coping skills that allowed for successful maneuvering through challenges historically experienced by African Americans at PWIs. Possible reasons for the difference in transition compared to traditional African American college students could rest in the critical thinking and coping skills acquired through home education. Past research on African Americans in PWIs has shown that these students resort to reactive and/or suppressive coping styles that lack critical thinking and often predictive of distress resulting in problems transitioning and persistence at PWIs (Lopez et al., 2001). The lived experiences of the participants of this research demonstrated that they were aware of options when faced with challenges and used proactive problem solving.

The homeschooled African American students of this study came into college with not only traditional but also nontraditional knowledge (service learning, multicultural activities, international travel); positive academic efficacy (self-confidence, utilizing study groups and advisors); long term academic goals; social awareness (ability to deal with racism, sexism, prejudices, and bigotry) that tend to hinder African American students at PWIs.

Limitations

The small sampling for this research study limited generalizations on the phenomenon, making the transition and identity development experiences of the participants not necessarily representative of all African American homeschooled students.

Notwithstanding, besides the inherent limitations of a small sample size, more consideration could have been taken in collecting more data on the dynamics of the participants' home education and curriculum.

Implications for Future Research

Implications for future research on formerly homeschooled African American college students' transition into higher education are numerous. State and national statistics of how many homeschooled African Americans are currently enrolled in four year brick and mortar institutions; their degree program choices; graduation rates; as well as how many furthered their educational journey and acquired advanced or terminal degrees and at which institutions are areas of future research. All of the participants stated that their mothers were their primary instructor. Inquiry into African American homeschooled parents, their motivations to homeschool, their pedagogy, teaching philosophies, and homeschool curriculums is essential.

There has been a plethora of research studies on how people utilize phenotypes to make inferences on stereotypes to impose upon groups of people, however, the majority of them focus on White on Black stereotype versus same race stereotyping/biases/assumptions, and subsequent discrimination and oppression based on physical characteristics. Participants of this study discussed at length their social experiences and challenges with African American students at

PWIs. Research on the transition experiences of homeschooled African American college students at Historically Black College and Universities (HBCUs) would add to the knowledge base, as well as a longitudinal study with a larger sample of African American Students who were homeschooled that included additional variables should be conducted in conjunction with informational research on the perceptions of faculty and administrators of formerly home educated African American college students.

Finally, with the expected growing population of African American homeschoolers applying to colleges and universities across the nation, an African American homeschooled student development theory is necessary. Dr. Sky Lark anticipates continued examination of this sub-population.

There has been a paradigm shift in regards to African Americans' allegiance in honoring the rough road to *Brown v. Board of Education* and the Civil Rights Movement for equal opportunity and access to public education. A movement has emerged within the African American community that questions the value of public education for their children with increasingly more African Americans taking ownership of educating their children and preparing them for higher education.

The rise in homeschooled African Americans will increase applications to colleges and universities across the nation. However, there is currently no existing empirical research on the actual numbers of African American homeschoolers now attending Predominately White Institutions. Challenges that this population presents to these institutions are in the area of curriculum, academic freedoms, teaching styles, and student development theories.

With the expected growing population of African American homeschoolers applying to colleges and universities, higher education has the responsibility to engage in research that explores the impact of this phenomena, the preparedness of this emerging population as well as address any potential challenges they may encounter in the college environment. Additionally, institutions of higher education would have the unique opportunity to learn about the success of the African American homeschooling population, which may in turn inspire and/or require curriculum, institutional or policy changes in the future potentially benefiting the successful transition of all African American students as well as the general student population at large.

This research contributed to the dearth of literature on the fast growing population of African American homeschoolers who will attend college with each year in America, making the inquiring of this research focus a resource in higher education student development and making it beneficial for college faculty, administrators and student affairs practitioners. This research provided insight on the unique challenges of African American college students who transitioned from homeschool education to higher education at PWIs.

In addition, this research continues the inquiry into the pedagogy and curriculum of African American homeschoolers. This research has added to the demographic scope of homeschooling research by examining the experiences of African American students, which has not been included in previous studies on the collegiate challenges and successes of homeschoolers. This study provided a platform for further critical study and empirical research on this growing sub-population in higher education. Exploring how African American homeschoolers transition into PWIs comparison to the experience of non-homeschooled African Americans fosters an open forum for scholarly discussions with potential for further research on the pedagogy of African American homeschooling and its implications for higher education.

Table 1 Participants

PARTICIPANT	GENDER	AGE	YEAR IN COLLEGE	COLLEGE ATTENDED	MAJOR
#1	Male	22	Sophomore	Military Academy Upstate NY	Engineering
#2	Male	20	Freshman	Christian University Southwest VA	Criminal Justice
#3	Male	23	Graduated	Private University Northwestern VA	Kinesiology/Music
#4	Female	25	Graduated	Christian University Southwest Ohio	Physics
#5	Female	22	Graduated	Urban University Central VA	Graphic Design
#6	Female	16	Freshman	Urban University Central VA	Mass Communication
#7	Female	20	Freshman	Urban University Central VA	Art Illustration
#8	Female	18	Freshman	Urban University Central VA	Anthropology

REFERENCES

Adams, T. (2005). Establishing intellectual space for Black students in predominantly White universities through Black studies. *Negro Educational Review, 56 (4),* 285-299.

Akbar, N. (2008). Na'im Akbar: Distinguished psychologist, 20th ABPsi president. In R. Williams (Ed.) *History of the Association of Black Psychologists*, pp. 407-415. Sage Publications.

Allen, W., Bonous-Hammarth, M., & Teranishi, R. (Eds.) (2006). *Higher education in a global society achieving diversity, equity and excellence.* Amsterdam, London: Elsevier.

Anderson, K., Howard, K. E., & Graham, A. (2007). Reading achievement, suspensions, and African American males in middle school. *Middle Grades Research Journal, 2*(2), 43-63.

Anglin, D.M. & Wade, J.C. (2007). Racial socialization, racial identity, and Black students' adjustment to college. *Cultural Diversity and Ethnic Minority Psychology, 13*(3), 207-215.

Ancis, J. R., Sedlacek, W. E., & Mohr, J. J. (2000). Student perceptions of campus cultural climate by race. *Journal of Counseling & Development, 78,* 180-185.

Anton, W.D. & Reeds, J. R. (1991). *College adjustment scales.* Odessa, FL: Psychological Assessment Resources.

Antonio, A. L., Chang, M. J., & Milem, J. F. (2005). *Making exclusive inclusive preparing students and campuses for an era of greater expectations. Making diversity work on campus: A research-based perspective.* The Association of American Colleges and Universities.

Apple, M. W. (2006). The complexities of Black home schooling. *Teachers College Record.* Retrieved from http://www.tcrecord.org

Artiles, A. J., Harry, B., Reschly, D. J., & Chinn, P. C. (2002). Overidentification of students of color in special education: A critical overview. *Multicultural Perspectives, 4*(1), 3-10.

Artiles, A. J., Kozleski, E. B., Trent, S. C., Osher, D., & Ortiz, A. (2010). Justifying and explaining disproportionality, 1968-2008: A critique of underlying views of culture. *Council for Exceptional Children, 76*(3), 279-299.

Astin, A. (1993). *What matters in college? Four critical years revisited.* San Francisco: Jossey-Bass.

Baker, R. W., McNeil, O. V., & Siryk, B. (1985). Expectation and reality in freshman adjustment to college. *Journal of Counseling Psychology, 32,* 94-103.

Baker, R. W. & Siryk, B. (1989). *Student Adaptation to College Questionnaire.* Los Angeles: Western Psychological Services.

Baldwin, J. A. & Bell, Y. R. (1985). The African Self-Consciousness Scale: An Africentric personality questionnaire. *The Western Journal of Black Studies, 9*(2), 61-8.

Bandler, R. & Grinder, J. (1975) *The structure of magic.* Palo Alto: Science and Behaviour Books, Inc.

Banks, J. A. (2004). Multicultural education: Historical development, dimensions, and practices. In J. A. Banks & C. A. McGee Banks (Eds.), *Handbook of research on multicultural education 2nd ed.,* (pp. 3-29). San Francisco, CA: Jossey-Bass.

Barnett, M. (2004). A qualitative analysis of family support and interaction among Black college students at an Ivy League university. *Journal of Negro Education, 73*(1), 53-68.

Bean, J. P. & Eaton, S. B. (2000). A psychological model of college student retention. In J. M. Braxton (ed.), *Reworking the student departure puzzle*. Nashville: Vanderbilt University Press.

Beeler, R. (1950). General Ray H. Beeler's opinion on segregation to Dr. C. E. Brehm, September 26, 1950. *President's Papers (AR-0006)*. University of Tennessee Special Collections, Knoxville, TN. Retrieved from http://trace.tennessee.edu/utk_brehm/18/

Belfield, C. R. (2005). Home-schoolers: How well do they perform on the SAT for college admission? In B. S. Cooper (Ed.), *Homeschooling in full view: A reader* (pp. 167-178). Greenwich, CT: Information Age Publishing.

Benner, A. D. & Mistry, R. S. (2007). Congruence of mother and teacher educational expectations and low-income youth's academic competence. *Journal of Educational Psychology, 99*(1), 140-153.

Bielick, S. (2008, December). 1.5 million homeschooled students in the United States in 2007. Washington, D.C: National Center for Education Statistics, U.S. Department of Education (NCES 2001-033).

Birnbaum, R. (2004). *Management fads in higher education: Where they come from, what they do, why they fail*. San Francisco, CA: Jossey Bass.

Blanchett, W. J. & Shealey, M. W. (2005). The forgotten ones: African-American students with disabilities in the wake of Brown. In D. N. Byrne (Ed.), *Brown v. Board of Education:*

Its impact on public education 1954-2004 (pp. 213-226). Brooklyn, NY: Word For Word Publishing Co.

Bolle, M., Wessel, R. D., & Mulvihill, T. M. (2007). Transitional experiences of first-year college students who were homeschooled. *Journal of College Student Development, 48*, 637-654.

Bonner, II, F. A. & Bailey, K. W. (2006). Enhancing the academic climate for African American men. In M. J. Cuyjet & Associates (Eds.), *African American men in college,* (pp. 24-46). San Francisco, CA: Jossey-Bass.

Bowditch, G. (2003). Homeschooling deprives children of important social lessons. In C. Mur (Ed.), *At issue: Homeschooling,* (pp. 61-63). Farmington Hills, MI: Greenhaven.

Braxton, J. M., Hirschy, A. S., & McClendon, S. A. (2004). *Understanding and reducing college student departure.* ASHE-ERIC Higher Education Report, Vol. 30, No. 3. San Francisco: Jossey-Bass.

Brint, S. (2006). *Schools and societies.* Stanford, CA: Stanford University Press

Brint, S., Contreras, M. F., & Matthews, M. T. (2001). Socialization messages in primary schools: An organizational analysis. *Sociology of Education, 74*(3) 157-180.

Bronfenbrenner, U. (1986). Ecology of the family as a context for human development: Research perspectives. *Developmental Psychology, 22*(6), 723-742.

Brower, J., Collins, T., Merry, R., Washington, M., Williford, E., & White, S., (2007). Emotional, social and academic adjustment to college: A comparison between Christian home schooled and traditionally schooled college freshmen. *Home School Researcher, 17,* 1-7.

Brown, C.M. & Yates, T.M. (2005). Toward an empirical corpus of historically Black colleges and universities. *American Journal of Education, 112*(1), 129-138.

Brown, R.A., Morning, C., & Watkins, C. (2005). Influence of African American engineering student perceptions of campus climate on graduation rates. *Journal of Engineering Education, 94*(2), 263-524.

Brown v. Board of Education, 347 U.S. 483 (1954).

Carter, R. L. (1955). *Legal background and significance of the May 17th decision: Desegregation in the public schools* (Vol. 2, No. 4, pp. 215-219). Berkeley, CA: University of California Press.

Casey, K. (1995/1996). The new narrative research in education. *Review of Research in Education, 21,* 211-253.

Cataldi, E.F., Laird, J., & Kewal Ramani, A. (2009). *High school dropout and completion rates in the United States: 2007,* NCES 2009064.

Chang, D.F. & Demyan, A.L. (2007). Teachers' stereotypes of Asian, Black, and White students. *School Psychology Quarterly, 22*(2), 91-114.

Chatmon, C. (2006). Exploring gender disparity in college aptitude among Christian college students from three school settings, (Doctoral dissertation), Regent University, Virginia Beach, VA.

Civil Rights Act 1964 Title VI, 42 U.S.C. § 2000d et seq.

Clemente, D. (2006). *Academic achievement and college aptitude in homeschooled high school students compared to their private-schooled and public-schooled counterparts*, (Doctoral dissertation), Regent University, Virginia Beach, Virginia.

Collom, E. (2005). The ins and outs of homeschooling: The determinants of parental motivations and student achievement. *Education and Urban Society. 37*(3), 307-335.

Conley, D. (2007). *Redefining college readiness*. Eugene, OR: Educational Policy Improvement Center.

Constantine, M. G., Wilton, L., & Caldwell, L. D. (2003). The role of social support in moderating the relationship between psychological distress and willingness to seek psychological help among Black and Latino college students. *Journal of College Counseling, 6,* 155-165.

Cottrol, R., Diamond, R., and Ware, L. (2003). *Brown v. Board of Education: Caste, culture, and the Constitution.* Lawrence, KS: University Press of Kansas.

Creswell, J. W. (2007). *Qualitative inquiry and research design: Choosing among five approaches*. Thousand Oaks, CA: Sage Publications.

Creswell, J. W. (1998). *Qualitative inquiry and research design: Choosing among five designs*. Thousand Oaks, CA: Sage.

Creswell, J. W. (2003). *Research design: quantitative, qualitative, and mixed methods approaches*. Thousand Oaks, CA: Sage Publications.

Creswell, J. W. (2008). *Educational research: Planning, conducting, and evaluating quantitative and qualitative research* (3rd ed.). Upper Saddle River, NJ: Prentice Hall.

Creswell, J. W. (2005). *Educational research: Planning, conducting, and evaluating quantitative and qualitative research* (2nd ed.). Upper Saddle River, NJ: Pearson Education.

Cruce, T. M., Wolniak, G. C., Seifert, T. A., & Pascarella, E. T. (2006). Impacts of good practices on cognitive development, learning orientations, and graduate degree plans during the first year of college. *Journal of College Student Development, 47*(4), 365-383.

Cushman, C. (2004). *Black, White, and Brown: The landmark school desegregation case in retrospect.* Washington, DC: CQ Press.

Cuyjet, M. J. (2006a). African American college men: Twenty-first century issues and concerns. In M. J. Cuyjet & Associates (Eds.), *African American men in college,* (pp. 3-23). San Francisco, CA: Jossey-Bass.

Cuyjet, M. J. (2006b). Helping African American men matriculate: Ideas and suggestions. In M. J. Cuyjet & Associates (Eds.), *African American men in college,* (pp. 237-249). San Francisco, CA: Jossey-Bass.

Darling-Hammond, L. (2007). Building a system for powerful teaching and learning. In *Building a 21st century U.S. education system.* Published by the National Commission on Teaching and America's Future and Bob Wehling (pp. 65-74).

Davis, F. J. (1991). The nation's rule, who is Black? : One nation's definition. University Park, PA: The Pennsylvania State University Press.

Decker, D. M., Dona, D. P., & Christensen, S. L. (2007). Behaviorally at-risk African American students: The importance of student-teacher relationships for student outcomes. *Journal of School Psychology, 45*(1), 83-109.

DiStefano, D., Kjell, E., & Silverman, R. (2004). *Encyclopedia of distributed learning.* Thousand Oaks, CA: Sage Publications.

Duggan, M. H. (2010). Is all college preparation equal? Pre-community college experience of home-schooled, private-schooled, and public-schooled students. *Community College Journal of Research and Practice, 34*(1/2), 25-38.

Durkheim, E. (1925/1961). *Moral education: A study in the theory and application of the sociology of education.* (E. Wilson, & H. Schnurer, Trans.) New York: The Free Press.

Egelko, B. & Tucker, J. (2008, July). Homeschoolers' setback sends shock waves through state. *San Francisco Chronicle.* Retrieved July 2012 from http://www.sfgate.com/education/article/Homeschoolers-setback-in-appeals-court-ruling-3225235.php#photo-2367793

Engstrom, C. & Tinto, V. (2008, January/February). Access without support is not opportunity. *Change: The Magazine of Higher Learning, 40*(1), 46-50.

Evans, N. J., Forney, D. S., & Guido-DiBrito, F. (1998). *Student development in college: Theory, research, and practice.* San Francisco: Jossey-Bass.

Fager, J. & Brewster, C. (2000). Making positive connections with homeschoolers. Portland, OR: Northwest Regional Education Laboratory. Retrieved from ERIC (ED 447 591).

Feenstra, J. S., Banyard, V. L., Rines, E. N., & Hopkins, K. R. (2001). First-year students' adaptation to college: The role of family variables and individual coping. *Journal of College Student Development, 42(2)*, 106-113.

Fields-Smith, C. & Williams, M. (2009). Motivations, sacrifices, and challenges: Black parents' decisions to home school. *Urban Review, 41*(4), 369-389.

Fleming, J. (1981). Blacks in higher education to 1954: A historical overview. In G.E. Thomas (Ed.), *Black students in higher education: Conditions and experiences in the 1970s,* (pp. 11-17). Westport, CT: Greenwood Press.

Flowers, L. A. (2007). Descriptive analysis of African American students' involvement in college: Implications for higher education and student affairs professionals. In J. F. L. Jackson (Ed.), *Strengthening the African American educational pipeline: Informing research, policy, and practice,* (pp. 73-96). Albany, NY: State University of New York Press.

Franklin, J. & Moss, A. (2000). *From slavery to freedom: A history of Africa-Americans,* (8th ed.). New York, NY: McGraw-Hill.

Fries-Britt, S. L. & Turner, B. (2001). Facing stereotypes: A case study of black students on a white campus. *The Journal of College Student Development, 42*(5): 420-29.

Fulbright, L. (2005, September 25). Blacks take education into their own hands. Once dominated by Whites, homeschooling appeals to more African Americans. *San Francisco Chronicle*.

Gay, G. (2002). Preparing for culturally responsive teaching. *Journal of Teacher Education, 53*(2), 106-116.

Gay, G. (2000). *Culturally responsive teaching*. New York: Teachers College Press.

Goodman, C. (2008). *'Home grown college students': An exploration of the epistemological development of homeschooled graduates in higher education,* (Doctoral dissertation).

Retrieved from ProQuest dissertations and theses database. (UMI No. 3327003).

Gordon, E. (2006). Establishing a system of public education in which all children achieve at high levels and reach their full potential. *The Covenant with Black America.* Chicago, IL: Third World Press.

Grant-Vallone, E., Reid, K., Umali, C., & Pohlert, E. (2003-2004). An analysis of the effects of self-esteem, social support, and participation in student support services on students' adjustment and commitment to college. *Journal of College Student Retention, 5*(3), 255-274.

Greer, T.M. & Chwalisz, K. (2007). Minority-related stressors and coping processes among African American college students. *Journal of College Student Development, 48*(4), 388-405.

Grinder, J. & Bandler, R. (1975). *The structure of magic II: A book about communication and change.* Palo Alto, CA: Science & Behavior Books.

Harper, S. R. (2006). Enhancing African American male student outcomes through leadership and active involvement. In M. J. Cuyjet & Associates (Eds.), *African American men in college,* (pp. 68-94). San Francisco, CA: Jossey-Bass.

Harper, S. R. & Hurtado, S. (2007). Nine themes in campus racial climates and implications for institutional transformation. In S. R. Harper, and L. D. Patton, (Eds.) *Responding to the realities of race on campus. New directions for student services No. 120,* (pp. 7-24). San Francisco: Jossey-Bass.

Harvey, W. B. (2008). The weakest link: A commentary on the connections between K-12 and higher education. *American Behavioral Scientist, 51,* 972-983.

Harvey, W. & Harvey, A. (2005). A bi-generational analysis of the *Brown vs. Board* decision. *Negro Education Review, 56,* 43-50.

Hausmann, L., Ye, F., Schofield, J., & Woods, R. (2009). Sense of belonging and persistence in White and African American first-year students. *Research Higher Education, 50*(7), 649-669. Spring.

Helms, J. E. (1990). *Black and white racial identity: Theory, research and practice.* Westport, CT: Greenwood Press.

Herndon, M. & Hirt, J. B. (2004). Black students and their families: What leads to success in college. *Journal of Black Studies, 34,* 489-513.

Holder, M. A. (2001). Academic achievement and socialization of college students who were home schooled. *Dissertation Abstracts International, 62*(10), 3311A. (UMI No. 302894).

Hoover-Dempsey, K.V. & Sandler, H. M. (1997). Why do parents become involved in their children's education? *Review of Educational Research, 67,* 3-42.

Hosp, J. L. & Reschly, D. J. (2004). Disproportionate representation of minority students in special education: Academic, demographic, and economic predictors. *Council for Exceptional Children, 70*(2), 185-199.

Howey, K. & Zimpher, N. (2007). Creating P-16 urban partnerships to address core structural problems in the education pipeline. In *Building a 21st century U.S. education system,* (pp. 87-98). National Commission on Teaching and America's Future and Bob Wehling.

Hudak, E. (2003). Public school is a better choice than homeschooling. In C. Mur (Ed.), *At issue: Homeschooling*, pp. 40-42. Farmington Hills, MI: Greenhaven.

Hurtado, S., Carter, D. F., & Kardia, D. (1998). *The climate for diversity: Key issues for institutional self-study.* San Francisco, CA: New Directions for Institutional Research.

Hurtado, S., Milem, J. F., Clayton-Pedersen, A. R., & Allen, W. R. (1998). Enhancing campus climates for racial/ethnic diversity: Educational policy and practice. *Review of Higher Education, 21*, 279-302.

Hunt, J. (2007). Making politics work to dramatically improve American education: Building a 21st century U.S. education system. National Commission on Teaching & America's Future.

Jones, R. L. (1996). *Handbook of tests and measurements for Black populations* (Vols. 1 & 2). Hampton, VA: Cobb & Henry.

Jones, P. & Gloeckner, G. (2004). A study of admission officers' perceptions of and attitudes towards homeschool students. *The Journal of College Admission*, 12-21.

June, N. L., Curry, P. B., & Gear, L. C. (1990). An 11-year analysis of Black students' experience of problems and use of services: Implications for counseling professionals. *Journal of Counseling Psychology, 37*(2), 178-184.

Karemera, D., Reuben, L. J., & Sillah, M. R. (2003). The effects of academic environment and background characteristics on student satisfaction and performance: The case of South Carolina State University's School of Business. *College Student Journal, 37*(2), 298-308.

Kim, D. (2007). The effect of loans on students' degree attainment: Differences by student and institutional characteristics. *Harvard Educational Review, 77*(1), 64-127.

Kirkland, S. L. M., (1998). Stressors and coping strategies among successful female African American baccalaureate nursing students. *Journal of Nursing Education, 37*(1), 5-13.

Klingner, J. & Edwards, P. (2006). Cultural considerations with response to intervention models. *Reading Research Quarterly, 41*(1), 108-117.

Kluger, R. (1977). *Simple justice: The history of Brown v. Board of Education and Black America's struggle for equality.* New York, NY: Vintage Books.

Kramer, B. G. 2012. *From homeschool to the community college: A multiple case study,* (Doctoral dissertation). Retrieved from ProQuest dissertations and theses database. (UMI No. 3506939).

Kranzow, J. M. (2005). *Taking a different path: The college experiences of homeschooled students,* (Doctoral dissertation). Retrieved from ProQuest dissertations and theses database. (UMI No. 3151767).

Kuh, G. (2005). Student engagement in the first year of college. In M. L. Upcraft, J. N. Gardner, & B.O. Barefoot (Eds.), *Challenging and supporting the first-year student: A handbook for improving the first year of college,* (pp. 86-107). San Francisco, CA: Jossey-Bass.

Kuh, G.D. & Hu, S. (2001). The effects of student-faculty interaction in the 1990s. *The Review of Higher Education, 24*(3), 309-332.

Kunjufu, J. (2005a). *Critical issues in educating African American youth. (2nd ed.).* Chicago, IL: African American Images.

Kunjufu, J. (2005b). *Keeping black boys out of special education.* Chicago, IL: African American Images.

Lattibeaudiere, V. (2000) *An exploratory study of the transition and adjustment of former home-schooled students to college life,* (Doctoral dissertation). Available from ProQuest Dissertations and Theses database. (UMI No. 9973466).

Lavoie, L. D. (2006). *Examining the perceived academic and social development of six early entrant home-schooled students in a Connecticut community college: A practical action research study,* (Doctoral dissertation). Retrieved from ProQuest Dissertations and Theses database. (UMI No. 3206629).

Levin, H, M., Belfield, C., Muennig, P., & Rouse, C. (2007). The public returns to public educational investments in African American males. *Economics of Educational Review, 26,* 700-709.

Lisle, V. S. (2006). *Analyzing the homeschooled student in college-level composition courses.* (Doctoral dissertation). Retrieved from ProQuest dissertations and theses database. (UMI No. 1444188).

Lopez, F. G., Mauricio, A. M., Gormley, B., Simko, T., & Berger, E. (2001). Adult attachment orientations and college student distress: The mediating role of problem coping styles. *Journal of Counseling and Development, 79,* 459-464.

Lubienski, C. (2000). Whither the common good? A critique of home schooling. *PJE, Peabody Journal of Education 75*(1/2), 207-32.

Marshall, C. & Rossman, G.B. (1999). *Designing qualitative research.* Thousand Oaks, CA: Sage Publications.

Martin, W. (1998). *Brown v. Board of Education: A brief history with documents.* Boston, MA: Bedford/St. Martin's.

Maxwell, J. A. (2005). *Qualitative research design: An interactive approach.* Thousand Oaks, CA: Sage Publications.

Maxwell, S. & Maxwell, T. (2008). *Managers of their schools: A practical guide to homeschooling.* Communication Concepts, Inc.

McDonald, S. D. & Vrana, S. R. (2007). Interracial social comfort and its relationship to adjustment to college. *The Journal of Negro Education, 76*(2), 130-141.

McLaurin v. Oklahoma State Regents, 339 U.S. 637 (1950).

Merriam, S. B. (2002). *Qualitative research in practice: Examples for discussion and analysis.* San Francisco, CA: Jossey-Bass.

Merriam-Webster Collegiate Dictionary (2013).

Moore, J. L., III & Owens, D. (2008). Educating and counseling African American students: Recommendations for teachers and school counselors. In L. Tillman (Ed.), *The Sage handbook of African American education,* (pp. 351-366). Los Angeles, CA: Sage Publications.

Morrill Act of 1890, Ch. 841, 26 Stat. 417; 7 U.S.C. Sec. 323. Retrieved from http://www.questia.com/read/23351526

Myers, L. J. (1993). *Understanding an Afrocentric worldview: Introduction to an optimal psychology.* (2nd ed.). Dubuque, IA: Kendall/Hunt.

Myers, L. J. (1988). *Understanding an Afrocentric world view: Introduction to an optimal psychology.* Dubuque, IA: Kendall/Hunt.

Nasim, A., Roberts, A., Hamell, J. P., & Young, H. (2005). Non-cognitive predictors of academic achievement for African Americans across cultural contexts. *The Journal of Negro Education, 74*(4), 344-359.

Negga, F., Applewhite, S., & Livingston, I. (2007). African American college students and stress: School racial composition, self-esteem and social support. *College Student Journal, 41*(4), 823-831.

Nelson Laird, T. F., Bridges, B. K., Morelon-Quainoo, C. L., Williams, J. M., & Holmes, M. S. (2007). African American and Hispanic student engagement at minority serving and predominantly White institutions. *Journal of College Student Development, 48*(1), 39-56.

Nemer, K. M. (2002). Understanding education: Toward building a homeschool research agenda. Occasional paper No. 48. New York, NY: National Center for the Study of Privatization in Education.

Nicpon, M. F., Huser, L., Blanks, E. H., Sollenberger, S., Befort, C., & Robinson-Kurpius, S. E. R (2006-2007). The relationship of loneliness and social support with college freshmen's academic performance and persistence. *Journal of College Student Retention, 8*(3), 345-358.

Nora, A., Barlow, L., & Crisp, G. (2005). Student persistence and degree attainment beyond the first year in college. In A. Seidman (Ed.), *College student retention: Formula for success,* (pp. 129-153). Westport, CT: Praeger.

O'Conner, C. & Fernandez, S. D. (2006). Race, class, and disproportionality: Reevaluating the relationship between poverty and special education placement. *Educational Researcher, 35*(6), 6-11.

Palmer, R. T. & Hilton, A. A. (2008, March). *A new paradigm to examine the academic disengagement conundrum among Black males*. Session presented at the annual meeting of the National Association for Student Affairs Professionals, Atlanta, GA.

Parade, S. H., Leerkes, E. M., & Blankson, A. N. (2009). Attachment to parents, social anxiety, and close relationships of female students over the transition to college. *Journal of Youth Adolescence, 39(2)*, 127-137.

Parham, T. & Helms, J. (1985). Attitudes of racial identity and self-esteem of Black students: An exploratory investigation. *Journal of College Student Personnel*. 26, 143-147.

Parham, T. A. & Helms, J. E. (1981). The influence of Black students' racial identity attitudes on preference for counselor race. *Journal of Counseling PSyCholo*. 2, 8, 250-257.

Parker, M. & Flowers, L.A. (2003). The effects of racial identity on academic, achievement and perceptions of campus connectedness on African American students at predominantly White institutions. *College Student Affairs Journal, 22*(2), 180-194.

Patterson, J. (2001). *Brown v. Board of Education: A Civil Rights milestone and its troubled legacy*. Oxford, England: Oxford University Press.

Patton, M. Q. (2002). *Qualitative research and evaluation methods*. Thousand Oaks, CA: Sage Publications.

Patton, M. Q. (1990). *Qualitative evaluation and research methods.* Beverly Hills, CA: Sage Publications.

Peer, J. (1982). *Lawyers v. educators Black colleges and desegregation in public higher education.* Westport, CT. Greenwood Press.

Pfleger, K. (2003). There is little evidence that home schooling is successful. In C. Mur (Ed.), *At issue: Homeschooling,* (pp. 55-57). Farmington Hills, MI: Greenhaven Press.

Phillips, C. D. (2005). A comparison between African-American and white students enrolled in an equal opportunity program on predominantly white college campuses: Perceptions of the campus environment. *College Student Journal, 39*(2), 298-306.

Piaget, J. (1972). *The child & reality: Problems of genetic psychology.* New York, NY: The Viking Press.

Plessy v. Ferguson, 163 US 537 (1896).

Princiotta, D., Bielick, S., & Chapman, C. (2004). 1.1 million homeschooled students in the United States in 2003 (NCES 2004-115). Washington, DC: National Center for Educational Statistics, Institute of Education Sciences, U.S. Department of Education.

Qaqish, B. (2007). A comparison of home schooled and non-home schooled students on ACT mathematics achievement test. *Home School Researcher, 17*(2), 1-12.

Ray, B. D. (2011). *2.04 Homeschooled students in the United States in 2010.* Retrieved from http://www.nheri.org/HomeschoolPopulationReport2010.pdf

Ray, B. D. (2009). Homeschool progress report 2009: Academic achievement and demographics. Home School Legal Defense Association, 1-7.

Ray, B. D. (2008). *Research facts on homeschooling.* Retrieved from http://www.nheri.org/Research-Facts-on-Homeschooling.html

Ray, B. D. (2005). A homeschool research story. In B.S. Cooper (Ed.), *Home schooling in full view: A reader*, (pp. 1-19). Greenwich, CT: Information Age Publishing.

Ray, B. D. (2004a). *Home educated and now adults: Their community and civic involvement, views about homeschooling and other traits.* Retrieved from www.nheri.org.

Ray, B. D. (2004b). *Worldwide guide to homeschooling.* Nashville, TN: Broadman & Holman.

Ray, B. D. (2003). *Facts on homeschooling.* Retrieved from www.nheri.org

Ray, B. D. (2001). The modern homeschooling movement. *Catholic Education: A Journal of Inquiry and Practice, 4*(3), 405-421.

Ray, B. D. (2000). Homeschooling: The ameliorator of negative influences on learning? *Peabody Journal of Education, 75(*1 & 2), 71-106.

Reich, R. (2005). Why home schooling should be regulated. In B. S. Cooper (Ed.), *Homeschooling in full view: A reader,* (pp. 29-42). Greenwich, CT: Information Age Publishing.

Reich, R. (2002, April). The civic perils of homeschooling. *Educational Leadership.* 56-59.

Reid, L. D. & Radhakrishnan, P. (2003). Race matters: The relation between race and general campus climate. *Cultural Diversity and Ethnic Minority Psychology, 9* (3), 263-275.

Rockney, R. (2002). The home schooling debate: Why some parents choose it, others oppose it. *The Brown University Child and Adolescent Behavior Letter 18*(2), 1.

Rosenberg, M. (1965). *Society and the adolescent self-image.* Princeton, NJ: Princeton University Press.

Rothermel, P. (2003). Can we classify motives for home education? *Evaluation and Research in Education 17*, 74-89.

Sachs, H. (1945). *Freud: Master and friend.* Harvard University Press, London.

Samuels, A. L. (2004). *Is separate unequal?: Black colleges and the challenge to desegregation.* University Press of Kansas. Lawrence, Kansas.

Saunders, M. K. (2006). *Comparing the first year experiences and persistence rates of previously homeschooled college freshmen to college freshmen who were not homeschooled,* (Doctoral dissertation). Retrieved from Peabody College for Teachers of Vanderbilt University, http://search.proquest.com/docview/305332234?accountid=14678

Schlossberg, N. K. (1989). *Marginality and mattering: Key issues in building community.* In D. C. Roberts (Ed.), *Designing campus activities to foster a sense of community. New Directions for Student Services,48,* (pp. 5-15). San Francisco, CA: Jossey-Bass.

Schlossberg, N. K., Lynch, A.Q., & Chickering, A.W. (1989). *Improving higher education environments for adults.* San Francisco, CA: Jossey-Bass.

Schlossberg, N., Waters, E., & Goodman, J. (1995) *Counseling adults in transition: Linking practice with theory*. New York, NY: Springer.

Seagraves, J. M. (2007). *I don't think about being a black student and going through school: An exploration into the development of academic identity in African American students,* (Doctoral dissertation). The University of North Carolina at Greensboro.

Sellers, R. M., et al. (1998). A multidimensional model of racial identity: Assumptions, findings, and future. In R. L. Jones (Ed.), *African American identity development: Theory, research, and intervention,* (pp. 275-302). Hampton, VA: Cobb & Henry.

Shealy, M. W. & Lue, M. S. (2006). Why are all the Black kids still in special education? Revisiting the issue of disproportionate representation. *Multicultural Perspectives, 8*(2), 3-9.

Sherman, S. L. (2012). *Case studies: African American homeschoolers: Who are they and why do they opt to homeschool?* (Doctoral dissertation). Retrieved from ProQuest Dissertations and Theses database. (UMI No. 1237999604).

Sidanius, J., Levin, S., Van Larr, C., & Sinclair, S. (2004). Ethnic enclaves and the dynamics of social identity on the college campus: The good, the bad, and the ugly. *Journal of Personality and Social Psychology, 87(10)*, 96-110.

Sipuel v. Board of Regents, 332 U.S. 631 (1948).

Sky Lark, T. (2012). The desegregation of higher education, race conscious admissions policies and the federal Constitution: Before Brown vs. Board and beyond. *The Journal of Pan African Studies*, 5(5).

Sledge, L. (2012). Get your education: Family support for African-American college students. *McNair Scholars Research Journal, 4(1), Article 6.*

Smiley, H. T. 2010. *She's leaving home: The effect of college experiences on homeschooled students*, (Doctoral dissertation). University of Arkansas at Little Rock, http://search.proquest.com/docview/750175167?accountid=14678.

Smith, C. E. & Hopkins, R. (2004). Mitigating the impact of stereotypes on academic performance: The effects of cultural identity and attributions for success among African American college students. *Western Journal of Black Studies, 28*(1), 312-322.

Solorzano, D. (2000). Critical race theory, racial microaggressions, and campus racial climate: The experiences of African American college students. *The Journal of Negro Education, 69*(1/2), 60-73.

Spring, J. (2010), *Political agendas for education: From change we can believe in to putting America first*. Routledge.

Steele, C. M. & Aronson, J. (1995). Stereotype threat and the intellectual test performance of African Americans. *Journal of Personality and Social Psychology, 69*(5), 797-811.

Steele, C. M. (1997). A threat is in the air: How stereotypes shape intellectual identity and performance. *American Psychologist, 52*(6), 612-629.

Steele, C. M. (2010). *Whistling Vivaldi: And other clues how stereotypes affect us*. New York, NY: Norton & Company, Inc.

Stenbacka, C. (2001). Qualitative research requires quality concepts of its own. *Management Decision, 39*(7), 551-555.

Stewart, E. (2006). Family- and individual-level predictors of academic success for African American students: A longitudinal path analysis utilizing national data. *Journal of Black Studies, 36*(4), 597-621.

Stokes, J. E., Murray, C. B., & Peacock, M. J., & Chavez, D. (1998). Cross' stage model revisited: An analysis of theoretical formulations and empirical evidence. In R. L. Jones (Ed.), *African American identity development* (pp. 123-140). Hampton, VA: Cobb & Henry.

Strayhorn, T. L. (2008a). Examining the relationship between collaborative learning and perceived intellectual development among African American males in college. *Journal of Excellence in College Teaching, 19*(2&3), 31-50.

Sutton, J. (2002, January/February). *Homeschooling comes of age.* Retrieved from http://www.brownalumnimagazine.com/storyDetail.cfm?ID=672

Swail, W. (2003). *Retaining minority students in higher education: A framework for success.* San Francisco, CA: Jossey-Bass Higher and Adult Education Series.

Swanson v. Rector of Visitors of the Univ. of Va., No. 30 (W.D. Va. Sept. 5, 1950).

Sweatt v. Painter, 339 U.S. 629 (1950).

Terenzini, P. T., Rendón, L. I., Upcraft, M. L., Millar, S. B., Allison,

K. W., Gregg, P. L., & Jalomo, R. (1994). The transition to college: Diverse students, diverse stories. *Research in Higher Education, 35(1),* 57-73.

Tierney, W.G. (1999). Models of minority college-going and retention: Cultural integrity versus cultural suicide. *Journal of Negro Education,* 68(1), 80-91.

Tinto, V. (2006). Research and practice of student retention what next? *Journal of College Student Retention, 8(*1), 1-19.

Tinto, V. (1997). Classrooms as communities: Exploring the educational character of student persistence. *Journal of Higher Education, 68(*6), 599-623.

Tinto, V. (1996). Reconstructing the first year of college. *Planning for Higher Education, 25*(1), 1-6.

Tinto, V. (1993). *Leaving college: Rethinking the causes and cures of student attrition.* (2nd ed.). Chicago, IL: University Press.

Tinto, V. (1988). Stages of student departure: Reflection on the longitudinal character of student leaving. *Journal of Higher Education 59*(4), 438-455.

Tinto, V. (1982). Limits of theory and practice in student attrition. *Journal of Higher Education, 53*(6), 687-699.

Tozer, S.E., Senese, G., Violas, P.C. (2006). *School and Society: Historical and Contemporary Perspectives* (5th ed.). New York, NY: McGraw-Hill.

Tyson, C. 2003. Epistemology of emancipation. In G. Lopez and L. Parker, (Eds.), *Interrogating racism in qualitative research, (pp. 9-28)*. New York: Peter Lang.

U.S. Department of Education, National Center for Education Statistics (2007), *Parent and Family Involvement in Education Survey of the National Household Education Surveys Program.*

U.S. Department of Education, National Center for Education Statistics (2003). *Homeschooling in the United States.*

U.S. Department of Education, National Center for Education Statistics (2003). *Parent and Family Involvement in Education Survey.*

Utsey, S. O., Ponterotto, J. G., Reynolds, A. L., & Cancelli, A. A. (2000). Racial discrimination, coping, life satisfaction, and self-esteem among African Americans. *Journal of Counselling & Development, 78,* 72-80.

Van Manen M. (1990). *Researching lived experience: Human science for an action sensitive pedagogy.* London, England: Althouse Press.

Van Pelt, D. (2003). *Home education in Canada: A report on the pan-Canadian study on home education 2003.* Medicine Hat, Alberta: Canadian Centre for Home Education.

Wallenstein, P. (2010, March 10). *Desegregation in higher education in Virginia.* Retrieved from http://www.EncyclopediaVirginia.org/Desegregation_in_Higher_Education

Wallenstein, P. (2008). *Higher education and the civil rights movement: White supremacy, Black Southerners, and college campuses.* Gainesville, FL: University Press of Florida.

Wallenstein, P. (2004). *Blue laws and black codes: Conflict, courts, and change in twentieth-century Virginia.* Charlottesville, VA. University of Virginia Press.

Weidman, J. (1989). Undergraduate socialization: A conceptual approach. In J. Smart (Ed.), *Higher education: Handbook of theory and research*, *5*, New York: Agathon.

White, S., Williford, E., Brower, J., Collins, T., Merry, R., & Washington, M. (2007). Emotional, social and academic adjustment to college: A comparison between Christian home schooled and traditionally schooled college freshmen. *Home School Researcher 17*(4), 1-7.

Wise, A. (2007). Teaching teams in professional development schools: A 21st century paradigm for organizing America's schools and preparing the teachers in them. *Building a 21st century U.S. education system* (pp. 59–64). National Commission on Teaching and America's Future and Bob Wehling.

Woodward, C. V. (1987). The case of the Louisiana traveler. In J. A. Garranty (Ed.), *Quarrels that have shaped the Constitution*. New York, NY: Harper & Row.

Yin, R. K. (2009). *Case study research: Design and methods*. Sage Publications: Thousand Oaks, CA.

Zimet, G. D., Dahlem, N. W., Zimet, S. G., & Farley, G. K. (1988). The Multidimensional Scale of Perceived Social Support. *Journal of Personality Assessment*, *52*, 30-41.

www.ingramcontent.com/pod-product-compliance
Lightning Source LLC
Chambersburg PA
CBHW041805160426
43191CB00004B/57